Permission to Laugh at a Funeral

Permission To Laugh

At a Funeral

Printed in the United States of America.

Edited by Melinda Port Cholewinski

Cover Design by Tosha Simpson

Published by Tosha Mills Simpson
reset.yourself@yahoo.com

Paperback ISBN: 979-8-218-30363-1

First Edition

Serenity Prayer

*God, grant me the **serenity***

*To **accept** the things that I cannot change*

*The **courage** to change the things that I can*

*And **wisdom** to know the difference.*

Tosha Mills Simpson

Life can be so beautiful... full of wonder, joy, and moments that simply take your breath away. But also, sometimes life can be really, really hard and it can tear your heart into a million pieces, leaving you to try and find a way to put it back together. Death can be even harder though, harder for those left behind anyway. It can defeat you, drop you to your knees, make you question and redefine everything you know about the world... but if you let it, it can also give you the knowledge, the insight, and the power to rise up from it in ways you didn't even know were possible before.

Simply put, death sucks! It just really does. But there is also a great deal of beauty to be found in those tender moments of our lives. This book is a collection of some of my favorite and most meaningful anecdotes from a brief period in my life where I lost quite a few of the main characters in my story. The interesting part of it though, and the part I am grateful for every day, is that I was able to somehow be present in those moments – to really feel all of the pain and to not only be aware of the transition happening from life to death, but to also really feel every ounce of love and enlightenment from that time too.

We all grieve in our own ways and for some of us, it's humor – even when that humor gets a little (or a lot) dark sometimes. It's that humor though, that ability to still find any joy in the heart of despair, that kept us going, and that made me who I am today.

I hope you will find these stories entertaining, uplifting, comforting, and inspiring. Remember friends, remind yourself that you have the power to grieve, celebrate someone's life, and most importantly, to handle death however works best for you.

Simply... give yourself permission to laugh at a funeral.

Hugs to you,
Tosha

Acknowledgements

First, please know that If I miss thanking anyone, I am grateful, just also sometimes forgetful. That said, I want to thank and acknowledge the following:

Everyone who has ever encouraged me to write, or connected with me about how my words may have affected or inspired them.

Everyone who supported this process – fielding endless options and helping me fine-tune everything.

My closest friends, for their patience, understanding, and grace during my withdrawn, starving artist phase, lol. *All the bits*

The incredible network of self-published authors and endless DIY resources online.

Shawn for being an amazing friend and partner in parenting. I am forever grateful for you.

My dad, *What a Wonderful World* you created for us to grow up in. Thank you for that! Also, for being an amazing friend in adulthood and an exceptional Pappy to the girls. I love you more.

My sister, Sierra for being the Disney to my NYC. For your honest, unfiltered opinions, and our "in the vault" conversations. You inspire me in so many ways!! You are my first and truest friend. I love you more.

Hailie for being the coolest kid. Keep dancing, singing, and embracing your weird self. It's up to you and Stella to teach your sister all the coolest trends, and of course some of the throwbacks. Goochie Goo.

Stella for being the most beautiful, kind, compassionate, hilarious human I've ever known; for understanding my need to make time to write; for being a beautiful and honest reflection of myself. Being your mom is the greatest privilege I have ever known! Lubba Loosha Loo, Bugaboo!!

Justin for coming along and pulling me out of my cave, making me laugh so hard, inspiring a new level of hustle, and teaching me the unlimited potential of the pivot. You have always made me strive to be the very best version of myself. Let's go!!

Melinda for inspiring creative freedom and storytelling as my high school English teacher, and more recently, for your help on this project - You and your 3,794 suggestions from commas and punctuation to "Are you sure you want to say that?" Your voice is so complimentary to mine, and I'm so grateful we were able to do this together. A million thank yous!

Dedication

Although I would much rather have the opportunity to sign a copy for her in person, it is my extreme honor to dedicate my first book to my beautiful mom.

Her words of support and encouragement were so strong while she was alive, that they're never very far from my mind, even years after her death. Growing up, she was always bragging about the accomplishments of my sister and I, and she was always amazed with our new endeavors. Her voice in my head telling me that I can do anything that I want to in this world has become a core belief of mine.

Sometime in the middle of heartaches and loss, the thing I wanted to do most was to put it all into words and to be able to share it with the world. What better way to honor her than to do the very thing that she was so good at doing – connecting people and reminding them that they're not alone; that brighter days are ahead; and that even in despair, joy is a deliberate decision.

Mom, I love you. I miss you. Know that we are well. Oh, and I wrote a book, no shit!

Permission to Laugh at a Funeral

CONTENTS

Permission to Laugh at a Funeral

Prologue

I suppose this story begins with my husband and I buying the house across the street from my parents in February of 2017. My grandparents had lived in that home for many years and had been looking to downsize and simplify for quite some time. We were ready to purchase a home and had wanted to relocate school districts before our youngest daughter started kindergarten in the fall. It was a win for everyone. I had helped my grandparents find this really cool little place tucked in the woods near a campground, with a river nearby. They were in heaven, and we were heading for our own new life adventure in their former house.

We bought it in February and began renovating most of the home. If I'm being honest with you, and so that you have a clear understanding of my mindset throughout this time – my marriage was theoretically already over long before we bought the house. We are both kindhearted people who divided household responsibilities really well and who co-parented like rockstars.

At the end of the day, though, and I'm simplifying of course, but the weird conversations I love to and need to have, were lost on him. In the same respect, I drove him crazy asking him to do certain social things that we both knew made him uncomfortable. We were different people at our core, and the marriage was not going to be sustainable for the long term. That house may have been our Hail Mary attempt – a fresh start in a new home, in a new school district for his oldest daughter, and our alma mater for both girls.

Having said all of that, throughout the renovation process, with many late nights and plenty of alone time working on the house to get it move in ready, I began to have a fair amount of quiet time to check in with myself and take inventory of where I was really at with it all and exactly how I was feeling. The more alone time I spent, the more I began to really feel like myself again.

In April of 2017, renovations were now underway, and my mom was diagnosed with breast cancer. I remember her calling like it happened just a minute ago. Her voice was shaky, and she choked out through tears, "Tosha, I have cancer." I remember feeling an incredible sense of calm wash over me - no fear, just calm. I took a breath and just said, "It's going to be okay. There's a purpose to it. You're going to be fine." And I meant it, though. I felt it in my bones that cancer was not going to kill her.

She turned out to be very fortunate. She was able to have a lumpectomy and radiation, and thankfully that was enough to heal her. Even in those dark times, though, my family who were already close became even closer, and the love we all had for each other just oozed out of us and swirled around like magic in the air.

We are the family who all showed up wearing matching shirts to sit in the waiting room during her surgery that read, "Hakuna My Tatas." The laughter and unfiltered conversation from that waiting room is what I remember from that day, ironically - no fear or doubt, just laughter, love, and togetherness.

I also watched as my sister's relationship with my mom softened quite a bit during this time and brought them to an even higher level of connection and understanding of each other. That was one of my favorite parts of that entire experience to witness.

One Sunday evening, the night before my mom's last radiation treatment, she mentioned wanting to go for ice cream sundaes after her treatment the next day. My family is also known for not missing an occasion to throw a party, and we happen to have the very best friends and extended family you could ever hope for! So, we got on the phone and called everyone to see if they were free the following evening.

Of course, they all dropped what they were doing to be there to celebrate with her. My Dad went with her to Ring the Last Treatment Bell. When they arrived home, there were about 30 of our closest friends and family there to celebrate the end of that chapter and to enjoy ice cream sundaes with her. The insane joy that radiated from her face as she walked in the door to be greeted by so many loving faces is the very best stuff in this lifetime.

That summer would end up being spent just enjoying and being grateful for life, and for each other. We laughed, we played, we were full of love and happiness. We were grateful everyone was healthy.

Below the surface, though, with every passing day, I became more certain that the intimate romantic part of my marriage had ended. As the fall set in, tensions in life were running pretty high. Things eventually came to a head one night. Taking the biggest deep breath, I took my ring off and respectfully told my husband that I couldn't do this anymore. Trying to get on the same page, meanwhile reading completely different books, was sucking the life out of us both. It wasn't the most surprising development, and honestly it was much more peaceful and amicable than I could have ever imagined. We agreed to keep the separation private, and to not even tell the kids at all until after the holidays. We wanted to take some time to wrap our heads around what comes next and to just enjoy the holiday season first.

It was at that moment, though, something inside of me clicked. I was about to genuinely reclaim my happiness. I was about to live a deliberate life again, one that made my heart smile every day. I remembered that I have the power to add or subtract elements of my reality based on how they make me feel. I have the power to be my most authentic self. At that moment, I made the conscious decision to embrace every moment of my daughter's youth and to give her the attention that she deserved and that I really hadn't had much energy or capacity for at that time.

Around the same time, in October of 2017, my grandfather began to have some health trouble. The VA Hospital he needed to be seen at was a couple of hours away, so I agreed to drive him and my grandmother so that he could have some testing done. After the first day of tests, we went to settle into the hotel for the night. All he wanted after that day was some KFC chicken and biscuits. I set out in search of dinner and returned a little later to have a picnic on our respective hotel beds while watching NCIS with them. It really was the most perfect little picnic, except for that part where I failed to make sure KFC included butter for those biscuits. Subtly, under his breath, I heard about that butter the entire time we watched that crime show and ate fried chicken. Adorably, with their bellies full, they were now tucked in and ready to call it a night... at 5:45 that evening.

That story is important because it was on that trip that I was first hit with the realization that somebody I loved was about to die. His results the next day indicated that he had an estimated 6 months to live. I may poke fun – but eating fried chicken in a hotel room and having forgotten the "damn butter for the biscuits" will be memories I forever hold onto.

The year before, I had made a road trip with my grandmother so that she could visit her sister when she was dying. When we arrived, it was clear that her sister was weak and tired of fighting. She had lost her siblings, her husband, and her son to cancer and so when she had been diagnosed herself, two years prior at the age of 82, she decided to tell no one. She kept it to herself and decided to spend her time traveling, visiting friends and family, and to just genuinely live like she was dying. It wasn't until her final days that her family even knew that she had cancer.

When we arrived to see her, my grandmother, who was her youngest sister, told her to just keep fighting and to not give up. When my grandmother and I were back at the hotel later that night, I found the courage to be completely honest with her and to help her realize that this would be the last time she would ever see her sister. We talked about how important it was to say goodbye and for her sister to hear from her that it was okay to be done fighting. That conversation deepened and changed our connection and unlocked a level of honesty and respect with each other that was so incredibly authentic and beautiful. She was able to agree with me and accept what was happening. The next day I was privileged to witness a little piece of her final conversation with her sister... so precious, so sweet. I smiled and winked at my grandmother before stepping out to honor their privacy and to let them have that moment together. Her sister died a few days later, only hours after her son was able to make it across the country to hug his mama one last time.

As for the fried chicken road trip... it was after that trip that I started being totally present and taking in each conversation with my grandparents, and parents, etc for that matter - those were my people. I was so blessed to have grown up with the kind of family who were also your genuine friends; the people you most enjoyed spending your time with; the people that understood you most and just brought so much good to the table. I now found myself asking questions, listening to story after story, hungry to hear all about them. I wanted to hear their history, their struggles, their triumphs... all of it. I was suddenly aware in each moment that it wasn't going to last forever, and I wanted to live in it as much as I could, for as long as I could. Not only did I want to savor it all, but I also wanted to continue the practice of clearing my mind to be as present as I could. I developed a sudden and strong interest in meditation, drum circles, etc. and was finding my peace, working my way back to my most authentic self with each passing day.

Permission to Laugh at a Funeral

Lost in the Holiday Spirit

And then came the holiday season of 2017. In light of my new awareness of mortality, and the fact that this would be our last holiday together as a family before the divorce, I had consciously, deliberately declared that I was going to make that holiday season the most memorable one ever! I slowed down, I did what I wanted and not what I felt obligated to do. I organized a bus trip to NYC for our community and took my daughter to see the city at Christmas. I was getting lost in her wonder on the daily and It felt amazing. I watched every movie on my holiday watch list, caroled through the town with about forty of our closest friends and family and even ended up running into the Grinch along our route! Unbelievably to my Grinch obsessed daughter, he accepted her invitation to come back to our house for cocoa, cookies and to take pictures with the kids! It was truly magical, every second of it!

My favorite part of that time came just two days before Christmas, bonding with my sister while making a special gift for our parents. We had talked for years about recreating old family photos and had just never got around to it. Almost putting it off again, on a last-minute whim we opened a bottle (maybe two) of wine and dug in. We chose our favorite photos, and ones that we knew we still had the props for buried somewhere in the archives of our parents' house. After a few glasses of wine and a trip down memory lane with the photos, we went next door and ransacked our parents' house for the actual pieces of nostalgia from the old photos. My mom lit up with excitement and wonder just watching us play and laugh together like we were kids again. My dad immediately guessed what we were doing! As we reached for the door with armfuls of old relics, trying to make a quick exit before specifics were noticed, we assured him he was wrong and tried to throw him off the scent.

We got back to my house and realized we needed a rubber duck for one of the photos. Naturally, we called a neighbor to borrow hers. She came in clutch with a bag of ducks and some top notch photography skills, as it turned out.

We quickly convinced her to have a glass of wine and to stay and be silly with us! Meanwhile, our parents were across the street, finding so much simple joy in what we were doing. We looked out the window once, only to realize that they were sitting on their porch, looking up at my bedroom window, trying to catch any sneak peaks that they could of what we had going on. Long story short, we had more fun playing and just enjoying life together that night than we had had in a very long time. Not only did we have a blast and create an amazing new core memory, but the gift turned out brilliant and we couldn't wait for our parents to see it!

At midnight on Christmas Eve, all of the boxes had been checked. The kids were anxiously waiting to see if Santa would bring them what they most desired, and for our daughter, that was a Power Wheels Cinderella Carriage. It was the thing she most dreamed of at that time. All of the traditions had been perfectly executed, holiday spirit was at an all-time high, everyone was healthy, happy and dreaming of sugar plums dancing. It was an innocent, magical time.

After everyone else had fallen asleep, I took a few minutes to just pause and breathe it all in. I sat alone in the quiet living room, lit only by the lights of the tree. I sat and smiled, reflecting on the past few weeks. I had set out to create the most wonderful and magical holiday of them all... and I had. I had been present, relaxed, and had done such a tremendous job at giving my daughter the experiences that great childhood memories are made of...

I should have rested my head easy, somewhere on Cloud 9 in that moment. I couldn't rest or relax though. I couldn't shake this overwhelming, impending sense of doom. Why had I felt so compelled to create the perfect holiday? Was I going to die? What if I never woke up?

It's important for me to explain that I am not someone who had ever struggled with depression and or anxiety. These were unexpected, unfamiliar, unsettling feelings that came out of left field. I tried to find a balance between trusting my intuition and rationalizing with myself that what I was feeling was probably just the symbolic ending of my family as I knew it, accompanied by the fact that my grandfather's health was declining. I told myself to try and just relax into the feeling of gratitude to be alive and to have just created such amazing memories and joyful experiences - despite being acutely aware of the fragility and unpredictability of life. It took me a long time to fall asleep that night. I just had this feeling I couldn't shake that if I fell asleep, I might not wake up the next day. Eventually I did fall asleep, though, and I awoke that next day to a joyful Christmas morning! Before going downstairs to open gifts, I took a deep breath and was consciously thankful for the day, and to be alive.

Permission to Laugh at a Funeral

Permission to Laugh at a Funeral

The Best Christmas Ever

The Best Christmas Ever started at sunrise with a very excited little girl finding herself on a silly scavenger hunt that would ultimately lead her to her brand-new Cinderella Carriage! We had invited my parents across the street to come over and share in that adventure - to experience the pure childlike joy bursting out of her. It was insanely cold that morning so no one stayed outside very long. We met up a little later that morning, though, at my parents' house, with my sister and her family as well. Everything about the air was different that day. The still presence and lack of urgency to do anything but just be in the moment, could be felt by everyone in the room. My mom was a bigger Christmas fan than anyone else I had ever met, so the holiday usually centered around her. Post-cancer maybe, I wasn't quite sure, but something about her joy that morning just captivated us even more than usual.

God love her, but she wasn't very good at keeping secrets. Her heart was pure and her mouth was honest, and so she didn't hang on to exciting news for very long without sharing it. This year was different. She had told me in a conversation months prior that she had gotten each of her granddaughters a secret special gift just from her and that she couldn't wait to give it to them. She never would tell any of us what it was, though. Christmas morning, that was definitely the first item up for business. She looked like a young child herself, literally bursting at the seams to give them their gifts. She very cryptically handed them each a small box and said, "this is your special gift from BB to remember me always." We laughed and joked at the darkness of the delivery, but understood her perspective, having just survived cancer. The gift was a crucifix necklace, identical to the one she wore that they all longed for and admired so much. She could not have been more proud to give them those necklaces, and they could not have been more happy and proud to receive them.

As we sipped coffee and relaxed that morning together, it became apparent to my dad that despite very clear, very insistent instructions from his wife that they were not exchanging gifts that year, she had a pile of gifts for him and he, in fact, had none for her. My parents had a love that far surpassed any love I have ever known. He loved and adored the hell out of her, but she was so incredibly insistent that year that he honor her wishes to not get each other anything, only to leave him heartbroken to discover that she went out and had bought gifts for him. He looked at me and asked me why I didn't tell him that she had gifts for him, and normally I would have. Mom had told me the week before Christmas that he was going to be upset that she bought him gifts. I asked her why she did that, why she told him not to do anything and then bought him gifts anyway. Her response sticks with me now forever. She just looked at me contently and said, "I really don't need or want anything. I'm getting him things that I know he needs and won't buy for himself." She seemed to know what she was doing, and really didn't want him to know; so I just filed it under 'not my business' and moved on with my day.

Her smile that Christmas morning though, as she sat in her favorite chair, seemed to indicate that she meant what she had said. She looked at him, smiled brighter than the sun, and said to him, "Honey, I was serious. I don't need or want anything. I have everything I could possibly ever want right in this room right now. Look around. This is the good stuff. And besides, anything else I decide I want; I just go buy anyway. So, believe me, I'm not wanting for anything right now," and she continued on just watching the kids open gifts with the most contentment imaginable.

With the kids playing on the floor in a pile of new treasures, it was finally time for the grand reveal of our last gift of the day - the recreated photo album from our childhood. Our parents sat down on the couch with so much excitement, and our dad instinctively just put his arm around our mom, as they looked at the album together. Each page brought more hysterical laughter than the one before and they were in amazement at the props, accuracy, and hilarity of the entire process. They were laughing so hard that I had an overwhelming urge to grab my phone and record it because it was just such pure joy. We captured on video, our parents sitting next to each other, reminiscing about our childhood and laughing so hard at us playing together as adults to recreate the photos. We had set out to give them this cool, unique gift - and in return they gave us an insane keepsake that my sister and I will both cherish forever.

After opening gifts, we had lunch together. We had talked about spreading out and keeping it casual but decided to make it a priority this time to squeeze in and have a now somewhat rare family dinner. We all sat at the table facing each other, eating and just having conversation together. My mom bragged about how her annual Christmas lasagna weighed in at an astonishing 15 lbs that year! We were together, full bellies, full hearts... it was perfect. It had indeed been the holiday I had set out to create.

After lunch we cleaned up and eventually went our separate ways. My sister was off to see her boyfriend's family and a little later we braved the cold again to take Stella for a quick trip through town in her new carriage! I was dealing with a head cold already and the air was just so bitter cold and intense that she and her dad finished the trip around town without me, while I headed back home. I popped my head into my parents' house for a quick second to tell them that Stella was on her inaugural adventure and loving every second of it! We quickly remarked on what a beautiful day it had been and agreed that we were gonna all lounge around and nap until my sister returned that evening to play some games and hang out a little longer. I said my "goodbyes" and "I love yous" as always and I walked back across the street to settle in for a quality nap and a little Christmas Story marathon.

A few minutes later, now back from her carriage ride, Stella came home and snuggled right in with me on the couch. As we laid there so cozy, watching a holiday classic, just about to drift off to sleep, I was reflecting on what a beautiful day, beautiful season really, it had been. Finally letting go of that feeling of impending doom and relaxing into the joy of it all, I couldn't help but think life was pretty damn perfect in that moment.

The perfection was short lived, however. Just before I was about to nod off, my phone rang, and it was my parents. I answered and heard panic in my dad's voice. He told me to come quickly. I jumped over Stella and off the couch in one leap as I asked if everything was okay. Remember, my grandfather had been in declining health and had already been given an imminent expiration. So, when my dad just replied frantically, "No it's not" to my question, I just ran as fast as I could across the street to him.

Permission to Laugh at a Funeral

The ~~Best~~ **Most Memorable** Christmas Ever

Fully expecting to hear him tell me that my grandmother had called with terrible news, I rushed into his house. What happened next though, I could never have predicted.

You see, in life it is rarely the thing we are worried about that gets us. Way more often than not, it's the sucker punch we never even saw coming that really knocks us off our feet. Twenty minutes prior to his call, I had opened the door to my parents' house, observed them in dim lighting, settled into their respective favorite chairs, watching a Christmas movie after enjoying a perfect day. We talked and ended with a typical I love you.

This time when I opened the door, I observed a very different scene. The bright overhead light was now on. My father was frantically pacing with the phone in his hand. My mother sat perfectly still, completely lifeless, and absolutely peaceful in that bright room, in her favorite chair.

I took one look at her and somehow knew that she was no longer with us. Honestly it was as if her spirit were standing behind her body telling me, "This is happening, but it's okay." My Dad called the paramedics, and I went to her to feel for a pulse, of course feeling none. I put my forehead to hers and just quietly said to her, "Seriously... you gave the girls 'special gifts to remember you by', but nobody thought that meant right now." I remember hearing my dad just yell out to her, powerless and desperate for her to respond to him. I didn't share that panic with him entirely; it genuinely felt much more peaceful from where I stood.

At that time the dispatcher on the phone asked us to get her to the floor to administer CPR, which we did of course, but I knew was completely unnecessary, even as we were doing it. In hindsight I'm glad that we did make an attempt to resuscitate her. Even though my Dad knew as well as I did that she was gone, it was harder for him to grasp what was happening. He had been in the room with her, powerless as she took her last breath, so suddenly and unexpectedly. I simply walked in right after. He needed that validation and reassurance that he had done everything he could for this person he loved most in the world. There was one brief moment as we were working on her, where the color returned to her face, and I caught a very quick glimpse of hope. Only to realize in the next quick moment that it was my breath that put the temporary color in her cheeks and as a result, took mine away for a moment at that awareness.

Although I don't remember, I must have made a quick call to my husband across the street, telling him to come get the dog quickly, and to come alone. He walked in the door to get the dog just before the EMT's arrived and I remember seeing his face as he walked in, completely unaware of what was going on. As he opened the door, saw us performing CPR on her, and realized what was happening, he just yelled out to her that he loved her and to keep fighting. Seconds later he was swept out of the doorway, with the dog, to make way for the paramedics who were now rushing in to our rescue. First in the door happened to be one of our neighbors. She locked eyes with me and had such a look of despair and pity on her face. She told me to go ahead and stand up, and as I continued chest compressions – having broken two ribs definitively during the process – I replied to her that I would get up when someone traded out with me. Just then, somebody was already jumping in to take over and I stood up to take a breath and call my sister.

I walked outside and remember feeling such guilt that I had to wait so long to call her. I told her the paramedics were there working on mom, but that she was no longer with us... or some version of that anyway. My sister was obviously in shock and we just kind of sat there on the phone in silence for a few seconds, like what the hell do we do now?! I also remember observing so many people showing up, but there only being an ambulance and one truck. It felt like a clown car full of paramedics had arrived. Later I would come to find out that time moves much slower in the middle of a crisis and that the elapsed time from me arriving at my parents' house until I finally called my sister was only two minutes and thirty-seven seconds! In my mind, twenty minutes had gone by before I got to call her; when in reality, it was less than three minutes.

As for the surplus of volunteers who showed up to help... as it turns out, our neighbors were in the middle of their own holiday dinner when the call came in. Quite a few people at that table were our local heroes who jumped into action and literally just came running. When I said it seems like 12 people just popped out of the bushes to come help, that is actually sort of how it happened. The fact that those volunteers left their holiday dinner to come to our aid has never been lost on me. It brought them into a completely different light for me and they have forever gained my respect.

They continued to work on her as they loaded her into an ambulance, while I gathered up my dad to meet my sister at the hospital. We arrived at the hospital and were ushered into the "Quiet Room." While we're on the subject, and no disrespect to the hospital, but the last thing I wanted to be was quiet and still. Lowkey, in those moments, I felt like my body might actually jump out of my skin. Those rooms would be much better served as a soundproof room with exercise equipment and fidgets for nervous energy. That way the choice is yours, but it accommodates everyone's needs a little better. That room filled up with so many of our closest friends and family that evening as we all sat and waited to hear what was happening.

That was a weird space for me to be in. On one hand, I had seen her. I knew definitively that she had died. On the other hand, we had been sitting there for a fairly long time if she had indeed arrived dead. So... as we all sat there sipping hospital coffee in awkward silence, I broke the tension and said... "Hey, do you guys remember that time Mom just died on Christmas Day?" It turns out that it was too soon to make that remark, but at least it had broken the tension with a few surprised gasps and then eventually a much-needed release of nervous energy through disbelieving laughter.

Finally, the world's most confusing doctor entered the room and sort of hopefully asked us about her medical history. My Dad gave him a quick rundown. He then told us what an amazing job the paramedics did, followed by silence and a kind of subtle and continuous head nodding. At this moment we all looked at each other in awkward and confused silence. My dad broke the silence and said, "and..." to which the doctor replied, "Oh, she's dead." Holy shit, man. Talk about terrible delivery. That guy was all over the place!

As the shock of the news settled in for a quick second, we went through the motions of first taking a deep breath and just absorbing and embracing that palpable love and support in the room, and then we made the walk back together to see her. Aside from earlier that moment when I pressed my forehead to hers as she was still sitting in her chair, this time with her was the first tangible precious moment that could have only existed in the middle of something awful. We had lost her. She got snatched up right out of our lives, just like that. Just like a video game where her character had died and now we have to keep playing without her. This was our last chance to really touch her, embrace her, to say an impossible, unplanned goodbye to her.

I don't remember specifics about my sister and my dad in those moments. My sister stood with her boyfriend, my dad stood there with his Dad. What replays in my head is me sitting down at her side, taking her hand in my hand, and holding it so long that it became warm and felt like she was really present and holding my hand - just for a minute. I remember that feeling and go back to it often when I am remembering or thinking of her. I will kind of give my thumb a little squeeze in my hand and breathe her in for a moment. That night at the hospital, I sat there holding her hand in my left hand, gently stroking her face and hair with my right hand as I said my goodbyes to her. For a million dollars I can't tell you what I said to her in those moments, but as I leaned in to kiss her forehead, I distinctly remember catching a whiff of a very unpleasant and unexpected smell. This was my first encounter with a deceased body, so I had no idea if what I was smelling was normal. I took a second whiff to try and figure it out, like we all do with unpleasant smells, right... and I burst into laughter. It wasn't dead person funk that I was smelling... it was parmesan cheese from that monster lasagna that she had been bragging about earlier in the day!! I imagined her wiping her forehead with the back of her hand as she cooked, which left her with the slightest powdery cheese residue left on the skin at her hairline. It was such a funny moment and a really great image to think of her happily preparing food earlier that day for what turned out to be her last family dinner with us.

As I stood up to let my sister have some time with her, I remember starting to break down and commenting that I would give anything for a great big Bonita hug. You guys... my sister's boyfriend, my now brother-in-law, came rushing over to me and grabbed me just like my mom would have. He held on so tight and never let go until I did. I became a life-long fan of his that night and knew that he would be the perfect addition to my sister's life. He more than proved that he wanted to plug right in and help take care of her, and the extensions of her. He handled unpleasant tasks that night with humility and confidence, and I will forever be grateful to him for holding us up during that time.

Eventually we ended our bittersweet goodbyes and headed back to my dad's house. My sister rode with me, and my dad rode with his brother. In those moments, my sister and I were both very matter of fact, and decided to handle the tasks at hand and make the calls in those moments, while we were still up to it. Looking back, that was such a cool time with her. It was at this moment that we entered into a new phase for the two of us; as newly appointed co-leaders, ready to work together and crush our first tasks at hand. When we got back to the house, I checked in with my husband and discovered that our daughter was sound asleep. I decided I would sleep at my dad's house that night, and that we would wait and break the news to her in the morning.

Permission to Laugh at a Funeral

Permission to Laugh at a Funeral

I Get By With a Little Help From My Friends

My Dad's house quickly filled up with our closest friends and family. Nobody quite knew what to say or do, but it just felt right to all be together. Again, it was so very cold that day, but now I just wanted to sit on the porch in my mom's usual chair. Two of my closest friends had shown up and neither one of them left my side that entire night. They went on to stay by my side, holding me up brilliantly that entire week, and truly it meant the entire world to me. That night on the porch, though, one was holding my hand and the other couldn't stop nervously petting my arm, in the very sweetest way, as she admitted that she just had no idea what else to do.

At one point I walked over to tell the neighbors, who were relatives and friends of ours. I walked in and told them what had happened. They both gasped in disbelief and shot up from their chairs, not knowing what else to do. They kept telling me to "have a seat, have a seat, sit down..." I just remember calmly telling them that I didn't need or want to sit down right now. She said, "You're in shock, sit down." I just smiled calmly and told her that I wasn't in shock but that I was just at peace and acceptance at her death. I went on to tell her that I would miss my mom like crazy and that I would feel the grief eventually, but that I didn't miss her yet. I had just spent the very best day with her, after all. This sticks out because I remember standing there that night, I remember my acceptance of the situation, and I remember knowing that grief would come, but it was not yet that time.

If we were handing out awards that week, my uncle would have gotten MVP for sure! He was an absolute rock star, and our rock for sure. He showed up at the hospital and basically from then on, never really left my dad's side. You'll see soon, but he also came in clutch on some special touches that ended up being pretty amazing!

Eventually we decided to try and get some sleep that night and did manage to get a few hours. The next morning, we were faced with the impossible task of telling our daughters. My husband and in-laws thankfully had gone to break the news to my stepdaughter the night before, but the little girls woke up that morning still unaware that their beloved BB was no longer with us. I sat down in the hallway and held my daughter on my lap. I told her that BB had died last night and that she had joined the angel club. Now she is always with us, watching over us and helping guide us, I told her. My beautiful, empathetic little five-year-old squeezed my neck so tightly and told me that she was sorry for me.

I went to the bathroom to compose myself and to breathe, and five minutes later she comes to me with a song she had just written for BB:

To the tune of
"We Wish You a Merry Christmas"
We wish you don't fall asleep again
We wish you a merry Christmas
We bless your heart
And a happy new year

Ugh! Tear my whole entire heart out! She was so peaceful and beautiful about the way that she handled losing her grandmother. It was really something kind of incredible. Later that day, standing in my mother's bedroom staring into her closet, trying to decide what we should have her wear for all of eternity... I finally really broke down. Stella looked up at me with big eyes and said, are you still sad about BB? I just sort of laughed at the innocence and peaceful bliss of being a child, and replied, "Yeah sweetie, I'm probably gonna be sad about BB for a little while." She put her arm around my waist and squeezed so tight with her little hand, as she assured me, "Don't worry, Mama; Everything IS gonna be alright." And in that moment, nothing could have been more reassuring than that tiny arm squeezing my waist as she leaned her precious little head into the side of my hip. In so many ways my own connection to my mother came flooding over me in that moment. She would often tell me that I was her rock and she would thank me for helping her feel better. I never fully understood it until that moment with my daughter's tiny little hand around my waist... the unconditional power and grace that comes from such a deep love, one like that of a mother and her daughter.

After telling my daughter that morning, I asked my husband to keep her occupied and distracted the next few days while I focused on the tasks that needed to be done. He would prove to be absolutely amazing and invaluable at taking care of her that week so that I could be with my family and not have to worry about parenting! After discussing logistics with him, I went back to my dad's that morning to face it all head on. I had a clipboard and notebook to keep track of everything. One of my dad's childhood friends worked for the funeral home, which made things much easier and more comfortable for us from the very beginning. She and I would go back and forth on details and she would playfully mock my clipboard, although it was obviously abundantly clear to everyone in the room that she had a healthy appreciation of and respect for my process. Ha! Ha!

At one point that day I had asked my dad a question regarding the after-service meal and reception. He suggested having it at my house, which was a modest home, large enough for a small dinner party – not large enough however, for 200 of our closest friends and family. Given that it was about ten degrees outside that week, a yard party was certainly out of the question. In light of that response, I just looked at him and asked him if he would prefer that I just figure out some of the details without him weighing in on everything. He actually put his hands against his stomach and pushed out away from his body as he told me, "Yes, please, just take that and handle it." I had so much respect for him in that moment, to be able to acknowledge that he was unable to take on that task. I remember just kind of laughing with him for a quick moment as we stood in his basement and briefly hid away from the world, and the intense reality happening upstairs.

We had so many amazing friends and family stop by that morning. One of my mom's closest friends walked in and brought a large coffee mug and a box of tissues. I'm pretty sure that she might have even still been in her robe? She opened the door and just said, "I've been up all night crying and it just felt right to come have coffee at this table." We all hugged it out and she spent the whole day just being near us, simply because she wanted to. My friends from the night before were there again, still diligent to my every need. Throughout that entire day, and days to come, we had the sweetest parade and steady stream of love and hospitality come through that door.

Permission to Laugh at a Funeral

So Many Decisions

We went to the funeral home that afternoon to discuss plans. Our uncle was with us and just genuinely held us up during this time. We had decided to have her wear her Christmas sweater, since it was her favorite day of the year, and coincidentally the day she left this Earth.

During the meeting with the funeral director, my uncle came up with the idea of having one last party with Bonita. Since our family is known for its epic theme parties, he suggested the crazy idea of asking the guests at the viewing to attend wearing their finest "ugly Christmas sweater" attire!! We all laughed and agreed that it was absolutely brilliant! It was just the kind of silly ridiculousness we needed in our lives at that time.

As we continued to make arrangements that day, we chose the serenity prayer rather than a more traditional Bible verse, when designing the funeral program.

God, Grant me...
*the **serenity** to accept the*
things I cannot change
*the **courage** to change the things I can*
*and the **wisdom** to know the difference.*

This was my mother's mantra in this life, actually. She believed in it so much that after an unsuccessful search to find the right piece of jewelry to have it inscribed on, she gave up and decided to have it tattooed on her entire forearm instead! It was also displayed throughout the house and quoted by her any chance she got. It naturally only seemed fitting for her to have the opportunity to remind people of it one last time.

When we got to the back of the program, we had the option of leaving it blank which most people do, or filling it with anything we wanted. It's important to know, that my mom said two words more than anything else in this world. "No shit." It could mean twenty different things depending on the context of the situation and the inflection of her voice. She would tell us often that from the time she was five years old, that was her signature phrase… and fifty years later it was still going strong. So, sitting in that funeral planning room, I'm pretty sure it was again my uncle who suggested, "What if you just write 'No Shit' on the back?" The room filled with laughter and we knew that was a right fit too! The result from that simple detail at the viewing would end up being just as classic as we had hoped it would be! People would go from crying to laughing after they flipped it over. It did its job, and it did it well! Sitting there in that room, strangely we were having fun and finding joy in planning this celebration. We made a custom play list also of her favorite music to play throughout the viewing. In the middle of complete despair, we were finding a way to make this fit us and feel good at the same time.

We went on to tackle the other important tasks and endless decisions that day and eventually returned home to more food than you can imagine. Our village was large, strong and just incredibly supportive!! One friend stopped to bring food that evening and laughed as she told us that the woman working in the deli made a suggestion as to what she should purchase because she had made several other platters that day and suspected that this one was making its way to our house also. Right there… that perfectly illustrates the beauty of small-town living! It has its quirks for sure, but when you need them, they show up!!!

When our friend from the funeral home gave me the generic form to use for creating the obituary, I took one look at it and knew that the summation of her life couldn't just be run of the mill, any more than any other detail of her final celebration. I took on the task of writing it and later that day I had set aside some time to get lost in her head, put myself in her world and connect with her essence to be able to write it to the best of my ability. In order to do that, I decided to go and sit in her bedroom, the place in this world that was just hers. I sat on the bed, took a moment to feel all of the things and to let them wash over me. And then I opened my eyes and I exhaled. The first thing that I saw was this plaque that read, "You have the rest of your life to be miserable, so enjoy today!" Damn. I knew she was maybe the most joyful person I had ever known, but I never realized what a conscious practice it had been for her. She literally woke up and started every day with the deliberate decision to find the joy.

Speaking of deliberate decisions, my family and I had quite a few conversations after her death about the beautiful, coincidental way in which her life had come to a peaceful end. She died on her favorite day of the year; she had spoken to almost everyone she loved and cared for so deeply, and those she didn't speak to that day, she had spoken to and loved on at some point in those final days.

In fact, one of our favorite funny memories came from seeing and visiting with her identical twin sister just days before Christmas. She and her husband had stopped by and we were all just smoking a little Christmas weed on the porch together. That night my mom even took a little puff, which she had refrained from for the past few months.

(I hesitated mentioning marijuana in this book, but the truth is, it would lack complete authenticity without it. Some people have a glass of chardonnay or a beer... I much prefer a little ganja if I'm going to indulge, as do more people than I could have ever imagined. After much debate, it felt important to include it in this story, and also to lend my voice to helping normalize it and eliminate the stigma from something that can be healing and relaxing for so many adults.)

Having said that, deep in the middle of that exceptionally fun session on the porch with everyone, I was joking with my aunt about using Tupperware as my motherhood inspired, scent proof, storage container. She didn't believe me that it worked that well, so I did a quick infomercial with her right there on the porch. I had her sniff the outside of the container and she smelled nothing. I then cracked the lid and as her entire face scrunched up as tight as it possibly could, she quickly pushed it away and could only manage to say "baaadd" through her sour expression. We laughed hysterically and continued just enjoying spending that time together.

For some reason, we all found ourselves a little more still and a little more present that evening. We shared nonstop laughter, nobody wanted the party to end, and there were insanely tight hugs all around when we did finally decide to wrap up the night. That is perhaps one of the most valuable life lessons I took from this time in my life. We always think we have time. You don't usually get to know when your time spent with someone will be your last time making memories with them; it just happens one day. What a gift it has been to just treat all of my encounters now, on some level, as if they are my last encounters with my loved ones.

But back to the peaceful, coincidental way my mom's life came to an end. We have affectionately joked that in so many ways it was as if she had actually died weeks earlier and just like in a Hallmark movie, she had lived such a rich life - full of kindness and service - that she was granted a little time to come back and beautifully wrap up her life this holiday season before she had to leave.

She set my dad up with "things he needs but would never buy," insisted he not get her anything and was joyful and pleasant at the realization that he had obliged her. She got the girls "special necklaces to remember her by." She got to sit with her husband as he put his arm around her and they just laughed and reminisced together on our childhood, and so many amazing memories. She cooked an amazing last meal and got to feed and spend time with her entire family. She lived her final moments like she lived so much of her adult life - creating deliberate happiness. For those reasons, it made accepting her death much easier for me. I knew immediately that I would miss her and that she had left a giant hole to fill, but I was accepting of her death, even from that first moment taking a glance at her from across the room. She left no stone unturned and always expressed how she felt. She had seemingly no unfinished business...

Well, except that it had been a goal of hers to climb a mountain and to proclaim with her hands in the air that she was a survivor, and to feel victorious in that moment, like she had finally overcome the traumatic events from her childhood. Sometime before her death, we had bought her a neon short and tank top set to wear when that moment came for her. She had it hanging on the back of her bedroom door, so she knew right where it was when she was ready for it. We decided that we wanted it buried with her, but we couldn't find it anywhere! We searched through every article of clothing in her house – and trust me when I tell you there were more than you can imagine, more than we knew, more than anyone knew. Yet, we found no sign of it anywhere. It had somehow disappeared. We now jokingly refer to that, and a few other familiar common items that were always in the same place and have now vanished, as being in "the box"- or the hypothetical, imaginary place we've created to explain their collective absences.

The ironic part of her wanting to climb a mountain and proclaim - with her hands in the air, that she was a survivor - is that she had, in fact, done that in some capacity. From the party we had following her last radiation treatment, we have a photo of her with the biggest possible smile on her face, her hands thrown high in the air with a sense of complete victory all around her! She had survived cancer, but cancer was only one small chapter in her life story. She had survived much worse than cancer at a much younger age. Her story really is one of unimaginable trauma. The only part of those horrific times that is relevant to this one, however, is that she was able to rise up from such heartache and despair and find a way to intentionally create joy every single day. She was more of a hero, and a genuine comeback story than you can possibly imagine!

This made it both easy and also challenging to write her obituary and her eulogy. When you have endless qualities and examples to choose from, it can be overwhelming to know where to start. When writing her obituary, I had the help of a very dear friend to talk me through it and decide on a starting point. I remember him talking with me about the way you just felt when you were with her. We spent a few minutes talking about the way that she made people feel and the connections that she quickly and easily made with them; and after that, it just expeditiously wrote itself. There was no greater honor than writing the summation of someone's life or the last speech that you will ever honor them with. Her obituary was entertaining, uplifting and most importantly, it told the story of her life. It highlighted the good stuff, relevant to who she was, and left out the boring, mundane, historical facts nobody really cares much about. It got to the heart of who she was and celebrated her spirit. Oh, and of course it ended with reminding everyone who planned to attend, that it was an ugly Christmas sweater party – our one last party with Bonita.

Bonita Joy Mills
May 1, 1962-Dec 25, 2017

What's in a name? Well, for this woman, a lot! Bonita translates to "pretty" in Spanish, and her middle name literally means happiness – pretty happiness, beautiful spirit.

Bonita was born May 1, 1962, in Altoona, to Starlette and the late Franklin Daski, alongside her identical twin sister, Wanita. So, if you're enjoying one of Bonita's favorite past times – shopping in Altoona – and start to think you're losing your mind, just go and say hello and share one of the many great Bonita stories with her!

Bonita, incredibly, was one of three sets of twins! One of the twins passed at birth, however her brothers, Duane, Wayne, and Greg, as well as Wanita, their mother and many other family members were still a big part of her daily life.

As a young adult, Bonita took a job at Proctor Silex in Altoona and set her sights on Bill. In her words, "I saw him, knew he was gonna be mine, and the poor guy never stood a chance." They have been together 37 years, very happily married over 34 years, absolute best friends in every way and genuinely the greatest love story of our time!

Bonita had two daughters, Tosha and Sierra, who loved her so much that they both moved in to houses next to their childhood home and started their own little village on the hill. She was also known as "BB" to her granddaughters: June, Hailie, and Stella, and loved these girls more than anything, which says a lot because she knew how to love fiercely! To June, she will be remembered for her listening and advice on life, and to Hailie and Stella, she will be remembered for the special donuts she kept stocked just for them and the countless hours they spent in her lap just curled up being loved by her.

Bonita knew the things we go our whole lives trying to figure out. She would go to Skip's for milk and be gone an hour, but the beautiful part was that she may have connected with several people and brightened their day while she was out. She was a kid at heart, a lover of Dooney & Bourke, a lover of the simplest things, a lover of life! She had a youthful spirit that just cannot be beat and that spirit lives on in the lives of everyone who was graced with her presence. Bonita was a great listener. She would let you talk as long as you needed about whatever you wanted, and undoubtedly throw her coin phrase, "no shit," in there somewhere. When you finished talking she would say, "give me a hug," and then honor you with the warmest embrace you can imagine.

Bonita was authentic, she was strong. She was humble and kind. In a word, she was "Bonita." She never had an encounter with a friend or family member that didn't end with an "I love you," or some declaration of just how she felt. She had no unfinished business, she knew to seize each moment and let you know just how special you were to her. May we all go forward and strive to be a little more like Bonita every day!

Until we meet again... We love you... more!

There will be a public visitation from 6-8pm tonight, Thursday, Dec 28 and from 11am to noon Friday at the funeral home.

The family has asked that those attending the visitation wear an ugly Christmas sweater for one last party with Bonita.

Permission to Laugh at a Funeral

Ugly Christmas Sweater Viewing

Then came the big day. She had died on Monday, and it was now Thursday. We were preparing to head to the Ugly Christmas Sweater Viewing we had planned. Still fun, but the realness and gravity of the situation, mixed with the sheer exhaustion from the week were setting in for sure. She looked beautiful in her Christmas sweater - so peaceful, and still so full of joy and contentment. We all sported our silly attire. But what happened when the doors opened – none of us could have prepared ourselves for. It far exceeded any expectations we could have had. The public viewing took place from 6-8 with a private family viewing from 5-6. Around 5:05 my sister and I look over to see the local gas station attendants coming into the viewing room. Her own mother had not even had a chance to view her yet. I had my sister quickly have the funeral director instruct them to please wait a little while until her immediate family had some time with her. They of course understood and were great about it. The funeral director was apologetic and told us she simply was unaware of who was family or not, and that most people don't come so early unless they are immediate family. We all had a collective quick laugh standing together in that viewing room about how our mother made everyone she came in contact with feel like immediate family - so much so that nobody was sure when to come to the viewing; it just all felt right.

So, with our first glances and rush of feelings out of the way temporarily, we opened the doors to be surrounded and embraced by the people that our mom loved and held so dear. And boy, were we! Throughout the next few hours, hundreds and hundreds of people paraded through the funeral home... and you know what? Almost every one of them had some completely ridiculous holiday outfit on!! It was the most incredible sight! Honestly, it became an endless parade of laughter at how everyone obliged and really rose to the occasion. All the while, her very favorite songs played in the background and photos of her were displayed everywhere, as well as scrolling electronically throughout the funeral home.

Funny sidenote about the photos... we did a quick gather of all of our digital photos of her, forgetting that when we had scanned them the first time years ago, there were a couple of photos you would definitely not want scrolling at your funeral. In the hustle of the week, though, those photos slipped through the cracks, until well... it was brought to our attention that, for example, the photos of her naked underwater in the pool, or the ones of her posing with a group of male strippers, were proudly scrolling by for all to see. Again, we just laughed and rolled with it. She would have just said "No shit" and went with it. Why should we give it a second thought at this point?

As my family and I stood there in line greeting everyone and just soaking up so much love, we listened to stories about how much our mother had counseled, preached to, and prayed with people…. endless people, on the daily. She had a whole life we really knew nothing about! We didn't need to though, that was the point. Even she may have been unaware of the extent of her reach. We just kept hearing, "Who will I talk to while I'm out walking my dog now?" or "I'm gonna miss our talks and quick prayers at the gas station," sprinkled in with an occasional, "Your mom brought me to Jesus." I mean, it was really something to hear.

Although it was amazing to hear everyone's love and admiration of our mom, it was hardly our favorite sentiment of the night. Two things took the cake for us that evening. The first was my mom's identical twin who had just lost her person in this world. Their bond was unmatchable and incomprehensible to most people. In order for her to cope with the evening… well - long story short - she was tanked when she arrived. She was an absolutely delightful, high as a kite, breath of fresh air throughout the evening. Completely innocently, but ferociously flirting with men in the receiving line – all as her patient and very understanding husband stood at her side. Important to know, she was all completely shit talking that night. She is madly in love with her husband and he is her best friend. Nevertheless, the constant stream of inappropriate but hilarious conversation that came from her all night was top notch. Her husband and daughter playfully assured us at the end of the evening that she would be in a different mindset the next day. Stay tuned.

What really stands out as our favorite moment of the night, though, is when this dear, sweet woman we have known for basically our entire lives, came through the line. She hugged me and struggled to find the right words to say, as don't we all sometimes in those moments? She stood in front of me trying to decide what to say and just sympathetically went with, "Oh honey, I'm so sorry. I didn't even know your Mom was sick." I said, "Thank you, and it's okay. She wasn't actually sick though. She had recently just been given a clean bill of health actually." Puzzled, she looked back at me, cocked her head to the side and said as if she were solving a mystery in her head, "Hmm... so, she just keeled over?"

Although I'm sure on some level my rational brain paused for a quick second at the oddness of the question, but it got quickly overruled by my auto pilot setting, and I just raised my eyebrows, nodded as I kind of snickered and replied, "Yeah actually, that's pretty much exactly what happened." She uncomfortably nodded and continued down the line. My cousin immediately walked up behind me, put his hand on my shoulder and whispered to me, "Okay... I know that you're not really retaining anything that is happening right now, but I promise in this moment never to let you forget, that there was a woman who directly asked you if your mother just killed over." We all burst out in hysterical laughter; and to this day... that is one of our favorite memories!

Sidenote... my dad ran into that woman months later and she started to apologize in total embarrassment. He just started laughing and told her how much joy that moment brought to us all. It now lives forever as one of the most hilarious parts of the funeral process... although it doesn't hold a candle to what would happen the following day.

Permission to Laugh at a Funeral

Every Time a Bell Rings...

Although exhausted after the viewing, I stayed awake that night perfecting the eulogy for the next day: a brief synopsis of everything she was and meant to me, in a short concise little package. Once I felt great about it, I got some sleep and started the next day with a pep talk in the mirror reminding myself how important it was for me to have that moment to honor her and affirming that I could get through it because it meant so much to me. As a backup though, a very good friend of mine had offered to jump in should I have needed him to... maybe an offer that simply gave me the extra confidence to take a breath and let it flow.

The time came to take our seats for her service that afternoon. There we were, seated in specific order, room packed with people... now it was real. Now it was actually happening; much less fun than the more jovial night before, but no less personal to her, to us, to our situation. The pastor began by reading her obituary and then sang the song, *When I Get Where I'm Going* by Brad Paisley and Dolly Parton. I was to follow his song with my eulogy. Except, until that moment I didn't know he was planning to sing. Music is my soul language – I can't help but feel all the things when I hear it... I thought, "Shit. Keep it together, don't focus on his voice right now, focus on your speech."

And then he sang the first few lines of the song:

When I get where I'm going
On the far side of the sky
The first thing that I'm gonna do
Is spread my wings and fly

... and I began to laugh, actually. The absolute most perfect segway came over me and I knew that I was going to be totally fine to deliver her eulogy with confidence and grace.

My dear sweet mother was pure of intentions, gullible to the extreme and just here for the present moment. She would be the first to tell you she never paid much attention in school and skirted by with the help of a collective effort from her friends, and of course the ability to switch identities with her sister. She couldn't be bothered with facts and statistics, but she was here for just about any conversation you wanted to have with her.

A few years before she died, she was in a conversation with her friends and one of them mentioned something about someone arguing that the world was flat, so she chimed in... "Well, isn't it?" Her friends shockingly looked at her, and gave a famous, "Bonita?!..." to which she would equally famously

70

respond, "...What?!" So that day, somewhere around fifty years old she got a science lesson from her friends that challenged her understanding of the world as she knew it. This became a well-known subject of playful teasing for years to come.

So, there I was, enjoying the rest of the pastor's song, and then he looked at me to see if I was okay to speak. I stood up with complete poise and approached the podium. I looked around the room and greeted the crowd by saying, "You know, I was just thinking as he was singing, that when Bonita got where she was going... the first thing that she did was turn around, take one look at things and say, "Hmm... No shit, how about that... the world really is round." Everyone burst into laughter, and in that moment, it steered the energy back to a more lighthearted space.

I went on to deliver the eulogy as seen on the next page. The song we had planned to listen to that afternoon wasn't cooperating with their system, so we skipped over that part and saved it for later. What a "trust the process" moment that ended up being though!

I closed the eulogy by pulling out a Precious Moments bell that my parents had received as a wedding gift 37 years prior and saying, "Please join me in quoting from *It's a Wonderful Life,* one of Bonita's favorite Christmas movies of all time... Every time a bell rings"...and as I choked it out through tears, they all joined me in finishing, "An angel gets their wings!"

With that, I rang their wedding bell to symbolize our beautiful mother getting her wings.

Eulogy on next two pages

Sitting down to write this eulogy was an honor and a privilege that I have both thought about and hoped wouldn't be for decades to come. I will admit, it feels a little like an 8th grade essay on who my hero is. Bonita was in a lot of ways her own kind of superhero. Her super powers were exceptional listening, contagious laughter, and the ability to spread love and positivity wherever she went. We have always known, but saw very clearly last night how many people's lives were touched by her. We have always said, when we grow up we want to be Bonita. She knew the secrets to life, the ones we often spend our who lives searching for, she just knew them. She lived life to the fullest, loved with every ounce of her being, never passed judgement, never criticized, never wanted to change you. She had a cup of coffee, a listening ear, and a hug for anyone who may have needed it. She saw beauty in everyone and everything and lived simply for the joy of life each day. She was stronger than anyone can fathom, and more gentle than anyone I have ever met. When trying to find the words to use today, I kept coming back to one of her favorite songs that she would often belt out at the top of her lungs... and rather than try to better express the sentiment, we would like to just play the song. Ironically this is the song Bonita used to use to describe her husband and later in life, her relationship with Sierra and I. Today, there are no better words to describe the way we view and reflect on our mother.

* Play Celine Dion, "Because You Loved Me" *

Many tears have been shed and people deeply effected by the absence of her presence in our lives. Bonita has always been truly an Angel here on Earth. Most interactions with her were you talking, her listening... and that can still happen. The warm love you felt from her, and that neighborly spirit... we can all go on to exhibit that from each other and continue the special way she made us all feel. In a way, although Bonita has evolved as a beautiful butterfly into the next stage of her life, she is still just as much here as she ever was. Close your eyes for a moment and take a deep breath. Feel the love in this room. Feel the warmth. Feel the spirit that was and will always be Bonita. Feel her when we stop and talk as we pass our neighbors, help someone in need, sit and listen when someone needs to talk, smile at a stranger, and spread love and positivity wherever you can.

Now, wrapping up this bittersweet holiday season and moving forward in love and laughter as we begin the new year, I want to quote one of Bonita's favorite Christmas movies of all time...

- *Remove bell and ring it*

"Every time a bell rings, an angel gets her wings."

Until we meet again, we love you... more!

Permission to Laugh at a Funeral

Permission to Laugh at a Funeral

If You Don't Know, Now You Know

As the funeral continued, one of our cousins paid tribute to my mom through song. She is an amazingly beautiful singer, who mostly uses her voice in worship. I had no idea what she was going to sing that morning, but as she opened her mouth and *Amazing Grace* began to pour out, I thought I would lose control.

When I was in high school, I lost two friends in the same unfortunate incident. At their celebration of life, the entire congregation, mostly filled with teenage kids, all sang Amazing Grace together. The energy, hurt, and anguish from that room, so many years ago, remains with me still. Every time I hear that song, I can't help but feel that pain all over again and shed a few tears. Ironically though, not that day. Our cousin sang the hell out of that song and did it every bit of justice! I couldn't help but let go of that decades old pain and just feel the love and peace in that room in that moment. It was a beautiful way to honor my mom, and it was a great addition to her service.

We then opened the floor up to anyone who wanted to share their favorite Bonita memory or story with us. We heard all kinds of amazing stories that day, but the one that stands out the absolute most to all of us, hands down, was her sister's tribute to her. Remember the night before when her husband and daughter assured us that she would be in a different mindset for today... well, they were right, but not in a way that anyone saw coming. God love her, she was the perfect storm of exhaustion, grief, a little weed and an Ativan. She got herself to the podium and her dear sweet mouth just did the rest.

She addressed everyone with a somber and sympathetic "You guys..." and kept just pausing to say "Bubbles, Oh Bubbles." Bubbles was her nickname for my Mom ever since they were children, because she was always known for her cheery disposition and bubbly attitude. When my aunt was finally able to really begin the eulogy, she first started with a painstakingly long story about being in school as young children and having to get shots. They were lined up, as identical twins (who, by the way, incredibly were one of three sets of twins born in their immediate family) and their mother worked in the cafeteria... long story short, they stood out. As she delivered her speech, some version of, "You guys... those shots, they fucking hurt," and "There were these double doors, and we didn't live far away from there..." and "So the shots, you guys... and the doors... and the shots and the doors..." Again, painstakingly long... long enough that I leaned over to my cousin and asked him to begin recording the audio of what was happening. To wrap up her story for you, they made a break for it, someone told their mom who walked down the street to get them, brought them back, marched them to the front of the line... and "You guys... those shots, they fucking hurt."

The audience was stunned at this point. She had just taken us on a little journey with her, and little did we know, we were just getting started. After a few smaller anecdotes and heartfelt sentiments, she just exhaled one more time and closed her speech by delivering the following beautiful gift to us all. She began to say...

"Murry." "You guys, Murry Christmas."

"Bubbles and I didn't say Merry Christmas, we said Murry Christmas."

Because, and I quote...

"You guys... Mickey's Twice Upon a Christmas... if you've never seen it, well you should watch it, it's a great movie. But we said Murry Christmas because in the movie, there's a reindeer and his name is Murry... and you guys, it's just such a good movie, no shit."

"So Bubbles, we love you. We're gonna miss you. Answer your phone in Heaven when I call."

And then she finished by driving it home with such complete conviction as she turned her gaze away from her sister and back to the crowd...

"And you guys... If you ever... get a reindeer.... Name. Him. Murry."

We were in complete shock, all 200 of us collectively at this point. She was never more proud of herself, and we were never more satisfied with a speech in our lives! Like I said, a lot of other people said a lot of really amazing things that day... but it's hard not to still be stuck on what to name my reindeer, should I ever decide to purchase one!

It took me a few weeks to call my aunt after the funeral, because I was unsure about hearing her voice; how similar to my mom's it would sound, and how I would handle it. One morning I was lost in grief though, and I called her. We had a great conversation. We laughed, we cried... and then I had to finally just come out and say, "Dude... your eulogy, what the hell?!" and we just burst into hysterical laughter until we couldn't even breathe. We broke down the eulogy and laughed for hours about it! It would end up being exactly the comic relief we both so desperately needed in order to begin muddling through how to move on without her in our worlds now.

Permission to Laugh at a Funeral

Permission to Laugh at a Funeral

Surrounded by Love

After mom's funeral service, we all gathered to enjoy a meal and live a little life together. At some point, my immediate family, joined by a small group of friends and family standing nearby, gathered in a huddle as the DJ played the song that we couldn't get to play during the eulogy. As we listened to Celine Dion's **Because You Loved Me**, we stood together in a circle in that banquet hall, and we sang and we cried, and we just held onto one another. When it got to the really high-pitched Celine Dion parts of the song, we just burst out in laughter remembering my precious mom who was the least musically inclined person that I knew. She never let that stop her, though! She loved to belt out in a playful, somewhat raspy, high-pitched squeal if the notes were out of her range. So standing there arm in arm, we looked at each other, threw our heads back, and let out our best imitation of her squeals – the way that she so lovingly and passionately sang that song many, many times. She loved that song so much. She said that it always reminded her of my dad, and the way that he loved her. In later years, she also felt that it described her relationship with us (her daughters) as well. That chilly Friday afternoon as we all stood together and sang that song, we now couldn't help but notice that every single word of it rang true for each one of us and how we all felt about her. I remember thinking as we swayed and belted out off key, how grateful I was that the music wouldn't play at the funeral home earlier. My takeaway from the experiences that day was to trust the process, to roll with the punches, and to have faith that there is a greater purpose, even when we're just not aware of it yet.

That dinner was full of so many sweet moments, honestly. Not one person was in a hurry to leave or to go anywhere else. We all just wanted to be close a little longer before we parted ways into a new and absolutely uncharted reality without her. The most beautiful moment from that dinner, though, is the one of the Bubbles Legacy. Remember I had mentioned that my aunt called my mom "Bubbles," which had carried over from her nickname as a child. Well, back in 1992 my aunt had made my mom a sweatshirt with a Precious Moments scene of a girl in a bubble bath on it. Written above the image was the word *Bubbles.* I loved it so much, that I insisted on wearing that sweatshirt to school one day when I was in the third grade. One day… in the third grade! My friend Mike thought it was hilarious and from that day forward, he exclusively called me *Bubbles.* Like a lot of childhood nicknames, it caught on, and soon many of our classmates joined

Mike in calling my *Bubbles* for the remainder of that year. As a matter of fact, that nickname not only lasted the remainder of our third grade year, but actually stayed with me until the end of high school, and even still for some people. Fortunately, my friendship with Mike stood just as strong as that nickname did all those years later!

As the end of our senior year approached, we decided that we were going to walk together as partners during our high school graduation ceremony. Right before we walked down the aisles in the auditorium and proceeded up onto the stage, I handed him the sweatshirt from all those years ago and told him that I wanted him to have it now. It perfectly symbolized the innocence of our youth, and it created such a cool moment for us - at a time when we were nervous and anxious, and needed that reminder of childhood simplicity most. He hugged me so tightly and then we took a deep breath and walked down that aisle, up onto that stage, and then out into the world.

Back to the post funeral dinner… both my aunt, who had made the sweatshirt, and Mike were there. Ironies of life, I actually ended up marrying Mike's oldest brother - so Mike was at the dinner both as my longtime friend, and as my brother-in-law.

Sometime after dinner Mike walked up to me, hugged me, and then handed me that *Bubbles* sweatshirt that I had gifted him right before our graduation in 2002. He smiled as he thanked me for letting him hang onto it for the past fifteen years, but then told me that he thought it belonged back with its rightful owner now!

Wow! You guys... get you friends like that! Holy smokes! It was the most beautiful, full circle of life moment I could have ever imagined, and I am forever grateful for it!

One of the very best parts of such a tragedy, and yes, there are allowed to be good parts... was the amazing blanket of love and protection we were surrounded with. We were privileged to the most wonderful outpouring of testaments people shared with us, food that was offered, sentimental cards, thoughtful gifts, etc. It was really something to experience that pure tangible love and ministry in action like that. Although it was the most difficult social gathering we had ever planned, we had found a beautiful, unique and fun way to do it in a manner that felt good and that worked for us. She wasn't standing in the room with us, but we had absolutely succeeded in having one last party with Bonita.

Permission to Laugh at a Funeral

Permission to Laugh at a Funeral

What Happens Now?

With the funeral behind us, we now awoke to a new emptiness that we weren't quite sure how to navigate. We were also faced with realizing that despite our grief and loss, the world had continued to turn, and it was not going to pause while we adjusted to our new normal.

Before the sudden passing of my mom, my husband and I had agreed to discuss the details of our divorce, and then act on it, after the holiday season was over. This didn't stop being a reality just because my mom had died, however my capacity for big life tasks was not huge at that time. We had a long conversation, and despite being clear that nothing had changed, we agreed that there was no immediate rush to put that all in motion during such an already trying time.

Also, obviously, that emergency call on Christmas Day was not in fact about my grandfather. Again, it's rarely the things we spend our energy worrying about that end up really being our biggest problems. He was still in declining health, though, and requiring more help by the day. He was such a prime example of how life continued to turn, whether we had the capacity for it, or not.

My entire heart was broken. I was adjusting to grief, I was living with, but privately separated from my husband, and I was helping my grandmother increasingly more and more with the care for my grandfather. My time and energy were in low supply, and what I did have was distributed as evenly as possible between running a business, being a mom, making time to grieve, worrying about my family and how they were handling everything, and actual hands-on caregiving for my grandfather.

One blessing that came from caring for my grandfather, was that it aided in a much smoother transition out of our marriage than many people are fortunate enough to have. My grandfather required more and more of my time as each day passed. Eventually I began to stay overnight a few nights a week at their house. This gave my grandmother a slight break, and also the opportunity to rest herself. Honestly, it felt good to just to be able to help for the sake of helping, and to spend that time with them too. I was very aware in those moments, that life is fleeting.

The new part-time caregiving schedule was actually incredibly helpful to ending our marriage peacefully, and in a way that minimized collateral damage to everyone. Shawn and I had many conversations about our situation and how it had not changed. There simply was too much life happening and I wasn't capable of one more major task at that time. Me spending that extra time at my grandparents' home gave us a sense of independence from each other and an opportunity to create a Mommy Night / Daddy Night concept and schedule that our daughter could start adjusting to while we were still living under the same roof. We spent many nights having conversations and learning when to stop for that day and when to start again. We had time, distance and division of labor. We were working our way toward a dream divorce. That is an absolute blessing that may not have been so easy if the circumstances were any different.

During those months following my mom's death, I had settled into being so insanely present in whatever was happening front and center in my world. I was never more aware that death was a certain part of life. And as certain as it was, it was equally unpredictable. None of us know when our time here will end. My family was committed to being even more present than usual, more affectionate, more purposeful.

While looking after my grandfather one day, I asked him what his final wishes were, what he would like to do most before he dies. That was its own powerful moment. Unexpectedly losing my mom gave us all a different awareness of death. In this situation, we had the gift of a little time to prepare for the inevitable, and to wrap up his life in a way that was calming and peaceful for him, and for us. His wishes were simple, really. He wanted to take a ride through the mountains, where he had spent so much time throughout his life. He wanted to have a family picnic and see his sons. And he wanted to rock out just one more time, the way he used to.

So, we set out to make those things happen.

First came the mountain ride. Just the two of us went. He was connected to an oxygen tank by this point, but several times during the drive he just took it off, stuck his head out the window and breathed it all in. Those months spent with him were such a gift to me. In a time when I desperately needed to slow down and look around, that's all he wanted to do. I was very happy and incredibly honored to give him that. He talked in great length about his time spent traveling the world and not being afraid of his next step, just trusting that there would be one, and that it would then lead to his next great adventure. In so many ways, that mountain ride paved the way for my next phase of life, as I would begin spending much more time in the woods and on that mountain.

My grandfather also wanted to get the family together for a picnic. Sidenote, in actuality he is my step-grandfather. My grandmother married him when I was approximately twelve. We don't do step or halves in our family though - if you're in, you're in. Having said that, we weren't able to coordinate his sons and their families from out of town with my grandmother's kids and our families... so we ended up having two separate picnics. First, we had my family over to their house for a potluck style dinner and all brought our favorite dishes and family recipes to share. A week or so later, he had four generations of the men in his family together for the evening. Both were magical times, soft and subtly somber, but also so full of love.

Lastly, it was his wish to jam one more time! He had always really loved to play the guitar, but he no longer had the stamina to play the way he really wanted to. However, their landlord, Tammy, (an old family friend of ours who owned the campground right next door with her husband, Ed) also happened to be the talent manager for Whey Jennings, grandson of Waylon Jennings. My grandparents were big Waylon Jennings fans and lucky for them, his grandson is an incredibly talented artist who puts his own spin on it, but is continuing, very successfully, in his family's footsteps! We were incredibly fortunate that she was able to convince him to graciously swing by their house on his next visit to town and do a little jam session on the porch with them. We surprised them with the visit one night, and you cannot even imagine how much they lost their minds when they realized who was at the door and what was happening! Whey, one of his band members, and Tammy, sat on the porch with my grandparents and jammed for almost an hour that night. Eventually, the adrenaline had kicked in and my grandfather was ready to take the guitar.

He managed to get a solid little session in before the adrenaline wore off and it was time to call it a night. I remember so vividly how alive and happy they both were that night. I remember how satisfied he was as I helped him get settled into bed. I remember thinking how deliberate and purposeful that experience was and how amazing it felt to be deliberately creating badass life moments!

Simultaneously, my dad, my sister and I were muddling through our new realities and how to pick up where my mom left off. My sister seamlessly carried on with the traditions and special little touches that were most important to the girls. My dad made sure to keep stocking some of their favorite treats that mom always made sure to have on hand for them. Me... well, I was helpful in a less conventional way. I suppose you could say the skills I had acquired in the fall regarding drum circles, higher meditation, etc. were proving useful now. After her death, I experienced a series of three very life-like dreams about her.

The unofficial host of my dreams was my great aunt Ann, my grandma's sister, who had passed away when I was around thirteen. She had actually appeared to me in dreams before this. The day after her own funeral so many years ago, I had taken a midday nap on the couch. During that nap, I dreamed that there was a knock at the door and I said, "Come in." She swung open the door, suitcase in hand and when I asked her what she was doing she simply replied with a big smile, "Moving in." I woke up startled for sure, but never felt any presence or activity from her in our house. However, when I was younger and would be driving, occasionally I would catch a glimpse of her in my rear-view mirror as if she was sitting in the rear passenger seat. An even crazier part to that story is that only in the last few years my sister shared the exact same story of occasionally seeing her in the back passenger seat while she would be driving! We had never talked about it until then, but we had shared the experience of feeling like she was along for the ride, ever present, and keeping us safe as we drove.

Now she appeared to be hosting my dreams. The first dream I had was one week after my mother died. My aunt Ann appeared to me in my kitchen, which of course used to be my grandma's before we bought the house from them. She hugged me; and my God, did it feel real. She took my hand and led me through my actual laundry room to what then became a different place. It was basically an empty white space with a door that she was protecting with her life. She said to me, "Oh, Honey, I'm so sorry to hear about your mom, you must miss her terribly." I told her of course I did. She replied with, "I bet you'd like to know how she is." I told her that I would like that very much. She said, "Well, sweetie, she's fine but she's just a little sad and can't really talk right now..." and then suddenly I woke up. I woke up crying that morning. Dream, spirit communication, imagination... whatever your belief, that was gut wrenching to imagine her alone and sad, and to be unable to communicate with her.

Two weeks later I had the second dream. This dream began with me suddenly appearing back at that door. This time I was alone on this side of it, so I knocked. My Aunt came to the door and quickly squeezed out of it, trying to prevent me from seeing or having any awareness of what was on the other side. I did manage to catch a glimpse, though, of what genuinely appeared to be an endless completely bright white hallway with an infinite amount of doors on both sides. I could also hear talking, laughter, music... It was joyful on the other side of that door, without a doubt. My aunt eagerly greeted me and excitedly said, "Oh hey, sweetie, are you here for an update?" She acted as if my visit was normal and expected. Confused, yet hopeful, I replied, "Sure." Her face lit up and she said, "Oh, she's doing awesome. But, she's so busy catching up with everyone that she can't really talk right now." Then just as suddenly as the first time, I found myself lying awake in bed. Holy hell! What a mind trip! Granted, I felt more settled and at peace after that dream than I had after the first, but I still felt like, damn... I've been to this door twice; can you meet me halfway already?

One month later I found myself dreaming again. This time both my sister and I were standing on our parents' front porch. In the dream we knew that Mom was already gone. It was very clear, actually, that she was there to say goodbye. There was a yellow jeep driving her, but I was never able to see the driver's face. We said our goodbyes then she hugged my dad, my sister, and I all goodbye, got into that jeep and drove off. My Dad was behind the storm door to their house, and we were still on the porch. We watched that jeep drive off until it was completely out of sight. When my sister and I turned around to join our dad in the house, we saw my mom standing right behind him. She was now also behind that glass, inside the house with him somehow. She looked at us, put her finger to her lips for us to be quiet and to not react, and then she perched toward him and waited with her hands in the air. Our dad took one step in her direction, gasped and froze with eyes wide open. She tapped her hands in the air at him and quickly and simply said, "Boo!" She then started laughing hysterically and said to us, "Nah, I really do have to go, I just wanted to fuck with you!" And when we all finished having a laugh together, she hugged each of us one last time and she faded off. I woke up that morning with a new sense of contentment and peace that I hadn't felt before.

My dad, a little salty that he hadn't dreamt of her yet and that I had, joked with me and asked if it had anything to do with the ganja nightcaps. I told him, it certainly might. However, to that point, if that was the thing helping me get to a place of open mindedness and enlightenment at that point, then I simply asked him in return if he would like some. The life lesson I learned from that was that we definitely don't always know why something seems appealing or compelling to us, but trust the process. Aside from my grandfather's diagnosis, I had no identifiable reason for wanting to become disciplined at meditation and thinking on a higher level that fall... until my mom died and then I had those amazing dreams. If even one tiny part of that had anything to do with my ability to be still and just listen, then that was a skill I was immensely grateful for, and also one I wanted to continue to sharpen.

Permission to Laugh at a Funeral

Permission to Laugh at a Funeral

Quiet Your Mind

Aside from dreams as a way to process what had happened, I was also seeing a counselor. As a benefit of my parents' insurance, we each received ten complimentary sessions. Although I didn't actually feel like it was necessary to help me deal with the loss of my mom, I figured it couldn't hurt. I did have a whole pile of other major life events happening at that time also and decided that I could use some of those sessions to help me sort through all of it.

This was my first experience with counseling in that capacity, for myself. I'm usually on the other end of those kinds of conversations. I found it easy to be vulnerable and real with my counselor, though. I treated it like she was a layer of my own subconscious that I had the rare opportunity to sit and talk with for a little while. It was not a terrible experience at all. I can tell you, we did end up talking quite a bit about things I would never have expected to talk about, though. Again, a reminder that it's often the things we never see coming that hit us the hardest sometimes.

I will forever be grateful for so many things I talked about and figured out how to solve in that room during those sessions. One thing we talked about was marijuana. She cautioned me not to numb my feelings or avoid thinking about them. I couldn't have agreed more with her advice. I explained to her, though, that it was exactly the opposite that was actually happening for me.

Every night after we moved in across the street from my parents, my mom and I would sit outside at night before bed and recap our days. We would laugh, cry, solve a few of the world's problems, then call it a night and start fresh in the morning.

That time outside at night became my meditation. It was my reset. Even without her there, it remained my sacred time to check in with myself and to give myself whatever I most needed in that moment. Some nights I would sit in silence, and some nights I would listen to music and look at the stars. Some nights I would write and be creative, and occasionally I would forget it all and just watch something on my phone and get lost in someone else's story for a little while.

I explained to my counselor, though, and it's one of the reasons that I felt so compelled to keep the authenticity of the story regarding the subject, that smoking a little weed on some of those nights did not make me unable to think about it all. Exactly the opposite was happening for me. I am a sociologist at heart. I want to understand people on a deeper level. I was no exception to myself. For the most part, I had experienced a picturesque, very happy childhood, but in those moments, I was feeling a lot of emotions that were new and overwhelming. And remember, the world didn't stop turning just because I was trying to grieve the loss of my mom. There were a million other thoughts running through my head at all times – my grandparents' health, my family's grief, my daughters, my marriage, my business, making sure lunches were packed and bedtime stories were read, clothes were washed, permission slips were signed, etc. Smoking a little weed didn't make me numb from those feelings. For me, it pushed all of those smaller details to the side so that I could solely create some time and space at the end of my day to focus on and sort through my feelings.

I went on to maintain some version of that routine consistently for years because it was so healing and important to me. Regardless of temperature, I would bundle up with a blanket and sit outside to clear my head on colder nights too. If you don't have some kind of routine, some time and space that you utilize, even occasionally to just check in and have a conversation with yourself, try it sometime. It just might be the best thing you've ever done for yourself. One of my favorite quotes in the world is by Ma Jaya Sati Bhagavati, "Quiet the mind, and the soul will speak." No truer words. Once we're able to drown out all of the day's mundane details, we are able to get to the heart of the matter and decipher what most needs our attention. Creating the time and space to learn that art is a gift I will forever cherish and be thankful for.

One night as I sat on the porch staring up at the brightest full moon, a thought occurred to me. I was experiencing loss in a way I never had before, and I was trying to make it make sense as it applied to my world. I had this beautiful metaphor come to mind equating the love I felt for my mother now - intangible but powerful and real - to that of an expecting mother, and how my own mother's love for me was felt by her before I was even born – intangible, but powerful and real. I stood up to get a better view of the moon and then took out my phone as the words just started flowing through me. These were some of my earlier days of knowing that writing was about to become a part of my future. Writing, as well as those nights spent just checking in with myself, and even the counseling sessions were all useful in helping me find some purpose and direction from that pain.

A Mother's Love
Written March 19, 2018

A mother's love begins the day she knows we exist. We are a part of her. She can't see us, or hold us, but she loves us fiercely. She talks with us, she laughs with us, she communicates with us on a level that you can only fully grasp if you have been blessed to feel another life moving through your body.

And over the course of your life, you grow and you learn about the world together. Through each other's eyes, as well as your own. You will love each other for your strengths and sometimes despise each other for the mirror image of your weaknesses. But over time, you will become each other's best friend. You will turn to each other for advice and lean on each other in times of need.

It may be unclear at points who is the child and who is the parent... and what a beautiful thing when they can be open, honest, and vulnerable enough to let us in like that.

And then one day they are gone... and a piece of you dies with them. You are left to redefine your life without them in it. This person who makes up half of who you are is now just gone. And it leaves a hole, an unimaginable ache. With time the aches become less often, but never less severe. Sometimes your brain tricks you into thinking that she is upstairs and will be down any minute... and then you realize that she isn't upstairs, and she won't be down any minute, and it takes you back to the moment that you lost her.
It feels as if you're hearing it again for the very first time.

But even in the depths of despair there are positives to be found. And my mom was really great at creating light out of darkness! For me, the light I am taking from this dark period in my life is that we now get to experience our mother's love fully and from every angle. We get to know her, to love her,
just as she loved us all those years ago.

We can't see her, we can't hold her, but we are connected to her, and we love her fiercely. We will talk to her; we will laugh and cry with her. We will honor her memory when we see her spirit in our smile and in the smiles of our daughters.
Our love has changed, blossomed, fully evolved.

For now, you see... where once I lived inside of her, she now lives on, inside of me.

105

Permission to Laugh at a Funeral

Good Shit Happens Too

The Millsketeers, as we began to call ourselves consisted of my dad, my sister and me. We were trying to find the fun in everything we did, and if we couldn't find it, we created it. We were recreating the things we most missed about what Mom had brought to our lives – her zest for life. The three of us went grocery shopping together once, not long after she died, which turned out to be hilarious! A grown man trying to do his grocery shopping with his two adult daughters pushing the cart... it was one for the books, for sure! We didn't just shop together, though, among so many things, sometimes we would meet up for a few drinks to unwind together and have a good laugh. We even found a way to make going through some of Mom's possessions a good time!

For the most part, my mom wore basically the same style every day. Black leggings or shorts and a t-shirt. She wore cotton nightgowns during the other half of the day. We knew she liked to shop, but it wasn't until after she died that we realized how insanely extensive her wardrobe was, especially for someone who dressed incredibly casually every day!

We found over $1,000.00 in clothes hanging in her closet, still with the tags on them! As I was going through some of it one day, I came up with a great idea! It was a long running joke that my mom was well-known for not hesitating to return anything, regardless of circumstance. She would laugh and say, "The worst they can tell me is no." In the spirit of those hilarious memories, I set aside all of the clothes with tags still intact. I did a little research and sorted them by the stores that they had come from and set out one morning to make the returns. I can't remember now, but I think we ended up with around $600.00 in store credits. I split the gift cards with my sister and told her that when she was really missing her most, to go and buy herself something nice, from Mom.

Later I went on to do the same. Specifically, I bought a necklace that made me feel empowered and a little like I was carrying her with me. It was pretty special to be able to receive a gift from our mother, even after her death. Thankfully her obsessive spending habits came in clutch and were able to be beautifully repurposed.

That new necklace would, soon after, be worn during one of my favorite life experiences from that time of grieving. My sister and I were celebrating our friend's birthday, and enjoying ladies' night out, listening to a band perform. *What's Up* by Four Non-Blondes had been one of our mom's favorite songs and the lead singer of the band that night had an amazing raspy voice that was perfect for that song. When the singer asked for requests, my sister walked up to request it. The band went on to play a song or two, as we all waited in excitement for our request to start playing. Again, she asked if anyone had any requests, and somebody yelled it out to her. She went on to play a few more songs and then took an intermission. As she returned from intermission, we walked up to her, told her how much we would love to hear her sing that song, and explained that it was one of our mom's favorites and that we had recently lost her.

Tears started streaming down her face because it was also her father's favorite song, and she hadn't sung it since he died, just a few days after our mom had. We hugged it out with her right there on the dance floor and then helped her get through that song – all of us together, surrounded by about a dozen other fierce woman in our circle. We all stood on that floor together and released a little of our collective pain through the power of that song that night... hand in hand, voices lifted, hearts restored. What a beautiful moment for everyone, and that singer conquered that song for the first time without her dad, in an unforgettable way. Ahh, I love the power of music, especially when it's live! Also, it was becoming increasingly clear to me by the day that bad things happen and are inevitable sometimes, but there is also good all around us, and if there's not... then the opportunity is on us to create it and to surround each other with love and joy.

For example, sometime in those first few months after losing my mom, another man in town died suddenly in his sleep, with his wife powerless by his side, exactly like my father had experienced. He died very early in the morning and around 9 or 10am I got a phone call with a proclaimed "unusual request." It was a relative of the deceased man, explaining that their family had noticed what a beautiful and unique tribute I had written as my mom's obituary. They were wondering if there was any chance I might be willing to tell his final story for them.

Wow! That moment is one I'll never forget. It stopped me in my tracks and made me feel both grateful to be seen and respected for my writing and also so incredibly humbled to be trusted with the task of wrapping up someone's life in a neat little package for them! Of course I said yes right away! I was crazy nervous, but was equally excited and up for the challenge!!

Honored by that phone call, I hung up the phone and did the thing we all dread doing after losing somebody. Filled with excitement and enthusiasm, right as I hung up the phone and pulled into work, I called my mom to tell her how honored I was. Ugh... gut punch! As that phone rang for the third time, the very harsh reality set in that my mother was not going to answer the phone. The irony of course, being that the very news I wanted so badly to share with her – that I was asked to honor somebody else as their life here had ended – only came as a result of me doing such a graceful job honoring her at the end of hers. I sat in my car and cried hard for a few minutes, then I sat there and, just like I said in her eulogy, I talked directly to her, feeling completely confident in her ability to hear me and rejoice with me in her own way.

Now the thing about obituaries is that they must be composed on a very tight deadline. In this case, it had to be at the newspaper's office by 10pm that night to make the next day's newspaper. I had stopped by the family's house quickly that morning and made arrangements to come back that evening after work. If I'm being completely honest, I had no idea what I was doing when I walked in that house that evening... but I had full confidence and faith that I would know once I was there.

Immediately upon entering I was greeted with an endless parade of warm welcomes. It was not uncomfortable at all. They were grateful to see me and eager to talk about him and to tell me his story. Soon after arriving, I settled into a spot on the couch, among kids and grandkids. I waited for a natural point in the conversation and then asked some questions that encouraged the family to share with me what was most important about him. It was surprisingly easy to get people to talk. After that session in their living room, I ventured out to the back porch to talk to his wife and some older relatives. I got completely different perspectives of his life from them, more pieces to the puzzle, more interesting stories... more of an idea about who he was and what was most important to him throughout his entire lifetime. It was such an interesting time in that house, having everyone surrounding me with his memories; it felt pretty damn amazing actually. Once I felt like I had enough information, and the anecdotal punch line that would make it flow and pull it all together, I left and went home to quickly begin writing it. Again, tight deadline to make tomorrow's paper. The words flowed out of me like I had always been meant to write them. After I was done, I sent the family a copy for them to review before submitting it. They were grateful and overjoyed with the final product! Weeks later a woman in town asked me if I had written this man's obituary. She said that she recognized the writing style from having read my mom's tribute. That was a beautiful day for me! What a cool honor to be recognized just by your writing style. Since then, I have actually written many obituaries, either for family or from requests just like this one. It's really the best gift I can imagine giving someone – a beautiful sentiment to their life, and it has been an honor being a part of each one!

Permission to Laugh at a Funeral

Permission to Laugh at a Funeral

Reflection in the Mirror

By this time, Spring was in full bloom, new normals were still being established, and life was marching on. We were adjusting to the best of our abilities. Although we certainly felt grief and sorrow, we were focused on living life in spite of the changes. For the most part, things were pretty joyful. My mom's birthday was approaching though, and it would be the first one without her. For a family of people who celebrate everything, what are we supposed to do now that she's not here to celebrate?! We still wanted to celebrate and honor her. After all, she does still have an identical twin, who deserved to be celebrated, as well.

We invited my aunt and her family for dinner and cake. We had also invited our core group of close friends and family to join us as we visited the cemetery for the first time all together to see her headstone which had recently been set in place. We took balloons for the girls to send up to her, and after my dad said a few words at her graveside, we had a moment of silence. We then released the balloons together. Again, horrible circumstances, but somehow we found ourselves standing in the middle of a circle of our people who were all showering us with love, and just genuinely happy to be with us in those moments. We are forever grateful to have friends and family who are always down for whatever we throw at them!

To celebrate her birthday, we shared dinner and a cake as we always would have, but this year, her sister blew the candles out for both of them. After dinner, after dessert, after the kids had gone to bed... we sat back on that same porch where just a few months earlier we had shared such a memorable time with my mom. I mentioned at the beginning that some families handle death with humor, sometimes dark humor... my family is one of those families. With full respect to all of the situations, we find the humor, even in the very darkest of times. This book would not be a genuine account of this time in my life if I failed to mention all of the dark, dark humor that helped us cope, make light of it, and get through it all.

Having said that... there we were, sitting on that porch on the night of their birthday. Kids asleep, Tupperware had been cracked wide open... Everyone was loose and having a good time. Suddenly we saw a man walking down the street. It's a small town. We quickly realized who it was, took an educated guess that he had been drinking, and as we saw him coming toward the porch, my aunt instinctively and without saying a word out loud, made the decision to have some fun with him. He approached us on that dark porch, knelt down to join the circle of chairs and started having a conversation with us. My aunt just sat there on that very dimly lit porch, looking at him with an entirely blank expression on her face. I just sat back quietly to watch this all play out, having no idea what she was doing, or was about to do. The man casually talked, as he was looking around the circle. When he finally glanced in my aunt's direction, she blanky looked at him and said in a voice I can only describe as a wobbly ghost impression, "I'm not really here… Nobody else can see me but you…" The look on his face!! Not one of us could contain our laughter, nor could we believe what was happening. This was the kind of joke only a surviving identical twin could get away with!

This set into motion the most ridiculous next hour of conversation! Somehow the conversation shifted to Halloween and the idea that my aunt should dress up as my mom. Remember, we live in a very small little town, while my aunt lives in a much larger area about 45 minutes away. For the most part she was out of sight, out of mind… or people who didn't know my mom really well, didn't even know she had an identical twin. We joked that since my aunt had longer hair, she should wear a short wig and put on one of my mom's signature cotton nightgowns that she always wore. We talked about setting the stage with my Dad set up on the porch, to hand out candy as usual. Then, whenever someone who we knew would appreciate the laugh approached the house, we would have her just casually walk past the door, inside the house, and walk right into the next room. Coincidentally, my sister had a Boxer that died a few months before my Mom did and that dog spent a lot of time with my Mom. Since my sister had recently gotten another Boxer, we discussed my aunt also casually walking the dog outside dressed as my mom.

Imagining people's reactions to those scenarios brought us all so much laughter that night! However, it only got more ridiculous from there! Once we mentioned her with the dog, we actually joked about having my aunt in costume with the nightgown and wig walk the new boxer around the block a time or two. As we all kept laughing and talking, the conversation got further and further off the rails. Walking the dog around the block turned into my aunt in costume, dressed in all white holding a bunch of white helium balloons walking down the street, with my dad walking a few steps behind her dressed in all black with his face painted like a frowny clown, walking with his head down! Even as I write this, I'm laughing at how hard we laughed that night, and how insane any of these ideas would have been if carried out!

Perhaps my favorite idea, though, was having my aunt visit the local bar dressed as my mom. The plan we schemed up that night on the porch was for us to casually go to the bar some night, nothing out of the ordinary. At some point, one of us would go to the bathroom and sneak my aunt in through the back door. We would return from the bathroom, sit down, and just wait. Wait for there to be a bar full of people, and wait for her to just walk casually through the kitchen behind the bar, so that you would only be able to catch a quick and fleeting glimpse of her; as she walked upstairs and out of sight, like it never happened. We couldn't stop howling, imagining everyone's reactions and how they all might stir with a sudden sense of discomfort and intrigue. Eventually we imagined my aunt walking through again and wondered if people would figure it out, or if we would have to have her come in for a grand reveal. No matter how we imagined it, it was epic and brought us nothing but joy and laughter in that moment.

Sadly all of those brilliant ideas remained just that... ideas. At some point later in that night on the porch, my aunt walked upstairs to use the bathroom. She came back to that porch with a look of pure horror on her face and said, "You guys... I'm done joking around. I was upstairs washing my hands in the dark because I couldn't find the light switch and I was 100% afraid to look in the mirror because I was afraid I would see Bubbles' face!" Of course we all lost it, and asked her, "Yeah but don't you usually see her face when you look in the mirror?" This was different, she decided... the joke was on her now, and she had had enough fun for one evening. With that, we packed the Tupperware away and called it a night! That night in the mirror was not her final deciding factor in why Halloween was a no-go... but we'll get to that a little later...

Permission to Laugh at a Funeral

Intentionality

While trying to find ways to be happy, heal and rebuild, I was actually really enjoying caring for my grandparents and spending that time with them! My grandmother and I had always been very close, and I became close with her husband, as well! They were not only family, but they were also genuine friends. I had so many amazing times with them over the years! They were simple people who just loved to be present and in good company! They were known for sitting around the kitchen table or a campfire, having a few beers and a little smoke. There was always room for one more, and you never knew when a jam session was going to pop up out of nowhere! Oh my gosh, what I wouldn't give for one of those round table jam sessions again!!

One of my very favorite nights with them included my best friend from college. She had come home with me for the weekend, and we were enjoying a typical evening with my grandparents. It started to snow, and before we knew it, there was a winter wonderland outside. At some point my friend, my gram, and I decided that we needed to take a midnight stroll through town in the snow. We put on our boots and gloves, and we headed out! Halfway through our walk, I stepped away for a minute to answer a phone call. When I turned back to rejoin them, I found them moonwalking backwards in the middle of the road in six inches of snow! It is not lost on me as to how fortunate I was to have had a grandma who was always down for crazy adventures and a good laugh!

Don't get me wrong, though... she brought her own share of crazy adventures and silliness to the table. While sitting at a campfire with her and my grandfather one night, they were rewriting and ad-libbing the words to the popular kids' folk song, *I Love the Mountains.*

I love the mountains.
I love the rolling hills.
I love the flowers.
I love the daffodils.
I love the fireside.
When all the lights are low.

Boom dee ah dah. Boom dee ah dah.
Boom dee ah dah. Boom dee ah dah.
Boom dee ah dah. Boom dee ah dah.
Boom dee ah dah. Boom dee ah dah.

The verses got more entertaining and amusing as the night went on. Finally, though, my grandfather proudly and melodically belted out, "I love a blowjob... on a Friday night..." Now pause right there for just a second. He was feeling so confident and clever, so proud of his lyrics ... until she quickly, without giving him a chance to go any further, replied as she snapped her fingers in rhythm and delight, "Except it's Saturday... so your lucks run out!" Hahaha! Mic drop right there at the campfire! His face when he looked so confused and then realized that she was right, followed by the two of them in hysterical, playful laughter together was one of my favorite life moments of all time! They weren't known for having material wealth, but they loved the hell out of each other and did have simple, endless fun together!

Having so many amazing memories with them, made it so easy to want to care for them and spend this precious time together. I sat and listened to many stories of his world travels, both while in the military and also for leisure and adventure. Especially during that last year with him, he couldn't get enough of sharing his story with me and telling me in vivid detail how beautiful different parts of the world were!

Also during that time, my gram and I had quite a few conversations about our family tree. She was the youngest of nine children and was the last remaining of her siblings. I know that had a great impact on her, along with losing her daughter-in-law and facing the loss of her husband. She was definitely much more 'seize the day' than ever before. She took quite a few mini shopping trips with my dad where they would laugh, play and both return with a cart full of the most random and unnecessary new treasures. Well, mostly my dad would do that, and she would playfully mock him for it and tease him that he had taken over his wife's shopping habits now that she wasn't here to do it anymore.

I forgot to mention the extent of my mom's spending habits. What I did tell you was that she had over a thousand dollars worth of new clothes still with the tags on them in her closet... what I didn't tell you was that literally, that was the very tiniest tip of such an unexpected and ginormous iceberg!

Let's skip back quickly to me going upstairs the day after she died to find an outfit for her. I opened her closet to a near endless, and definitely unexpected and overwhelming selection of possible choices. There was also another closet, two dressers, and a portable closet also filled with her clothes. I remember saying to my dad, playfully at one point, to just not even look into it any further, that we would take care of it. At some point while getting ready for the funeral, he walked past the spare room with that portable closet open and asked, "Is that whole thing filled with her clothes too?!" and looked at me in complete shock! I just laughed and told him I had warned him. He continued, "Do you know I'm over here struggling to fit my clothes in one dresser and she has all of this space filled with clothes she never even wore." Using that dark humor to lighten the mood... I just winked and replied, "Yeah, but it's all yours now. You can spread your clothes out as much as you want."

The effects of her spending continued after death, even. I believe it was the second morning after she had died, when one of our friends had gone to the post office to pick up the mail for us and returned with a package my mom had ordered before the holidays. We all laughed and wondered how many more packages might arrive that next week, and just how much the postal system would miss her now that she was gone! We did receive a couple more packages in the following weeks, if I remember correctly. While cleaning out some of her things we realized just how many packages had been delivered over the years. Not only did she have an unbelievable amount of clothes, but she had also just as many shoes – literally anything you can imagine: dress boots, hiking boots, snow boots, casual boots, sandals in every color, sneakers, no shit – 10 unopened pairs of her favorite flip flop, I assume in case they ever stop selling them suddenly.

We also discovered a crazy amount of Vera Bradley complete luggage travel sets, and an actual insane amount of designer purses and complete coordinating sets – wallet, change purse, etc!   We. Had. Literally. No. Idea!!

My favorite posthumous find though, was the Temptations cookware. There were two complete sets... I'm talking full-service sets for 16 people of Temptations cookware, dishes and silverware! What was her plan?? We eat from paper plates at our family meals! Why did she have top of the line cookware and serving ware just stashed in the spare room still in boxes, as if it doesn't exist. Mysteries of life, no doubt!

But now you understand why my gram would playfully mock her son about taking over his wife's spending habits on those trips together. My dad and his mom were spending so much quality time together, and it was such a beautiful thing. He had just lost his wife & absolute best friend in this world. Dinner, shopping, and quality time with his mom was exactly what he needed most at that time. As it turned out, it was exactly what she needed at that time too. It was the perfect distraction for her, from the hard reality that her husband was dying.

Watching those two enjoy their time together, and spending my own bittersweet, reflective time with my grandparents, as my grandfather declined, reminded me of so many other moments with them. I was also never more aware that any of these moments could be our last ones all together. That period of time forced me to be present and motivated me to soak up as much as I could. The ability to be present in the each moment, whether good or not so good, was a gift at that time. When so many people get lost in grief and held hostage in the past, I felt as if I were experiencing life with a completely open perspective and the acute knowledge of just how fragile and unexpected it all can be... and because of that, I wasn't missing a moment of anything that was happening. Life, human connections, our people... that is the good stuff. At the end of the day, it's the only stuff that has ever really mattered to me anyway!

Permission to Laugh at a Funeral

The Sweetest Surprise

I haven't always been especially close with some of my mom's family, and geographically, some of them live quite far from us. I will admit that after that first birthday without her, though, I did find myself really wanting to connect with them. I found myself wanting to see those familiar pieces and extensions of her life. Coincidentally, around that same time, my mom's uncle reached out and invited us for dinner at the country club he belongs to. Excited to see some of her family and to connect with them - my Dad, my sister, our daughters and I met them for dinner. A few minutes into catching up, as we were waiting to take our turn at this amazing buffet prepared for us, the doors to the room we were in opened up... and in walked the rest of my mom's family!! Her uncle had surprised us and flown them in so we could all be together! It was truly overwhelming, in the very best way. My heart didn't know quite how much I needed to see them, but apparently our Great Uncle did. His generosity in bringing everyone together at that time will never be forgotten, and it was the beginning of establishing new relationships with each other on a deeper level than before.

We took full advantage of that opportunity, as we just sat and talked and laughed together for hours. We had last seen one another at the funeral (five months ago), but nobody had enjoyed the visit then. We were just existing together in autopilot. This time was so different. Everyone was relaxed, so present, and just genuinely sharing time and space together because we all loved this woman so much. We all needed to fill that void in our lives a little with the company and fellowship of each other in that time. Needless to say, we had an amazing evening together. We laughed, we cried, and we caught up on each other's lives. Before we ended the night, we made sure to take a group photo together. The best part, however, was that we would be seeing each other again the next day, before they had to leave to go home.

That next evening the family met at my dad's house so that we could all visit the graveside together. Her family had not had the opportunity to see the headstone and view her final resting place yet. So, on that gorgeous afternoon in May we all got together again to have lunch and to spend a little more time together.

Before our journey to the cemetery, my aunt asked if I wanted to sneak across the street to my house quick to "peak at the Tupperware." Of course, I obliged her. I didn't want to be rude, after all. This time, I took a wild shot in the dark and asked my grandmother to take a walk with us. She surprisingly followed us, and we asked her if she wanted a hit before we left for the cemetery. She responded that she wasn't sure, only because it might mess with her blood sugar levels. Confused, I looked at her and told her I was pretty sure it wouldn't affect that. When I walked out with the Tupperware containter, it all became clear to her! She was mistaken, and somehow thought we were doing shots of alcohol. I assured her that the marijuana wouldn't change her blood sugar level and she eagerly took it from me and hit that bowl like a champ, without any hesitation! I'm not sure who was more surprised... my grandmother, my aunt or me?! I'm known for pushing the envelope, so of course I had to try... but never in a million years did I expect it to work!!

My grandmother had taken two puffs before deciding she had had enough. Between bouts of hysterical laughter from all three of us, I asked her when the last time she had smoked was, and she quickly replied, "Oh, I never have." You guys... to be clear, my 80-year-old grandmother is standing on my porch having just hit the bowl twice and then tells me this is her first time... ever!! We laughed so hard we couldn't breathe. All we could imagine was my mom standing there with us and how in shock she would have been! How in shock, but how filled with love to see everyone just living and laughing together.

We packed the Tupperware away and caravanned with the rest of the family to the cemetery. In the maybe fifteen minutes that had elapsed, my grandmother was well on her way to having a very good afternoon. That quick trip to the porch was exactly what she had needed, what we all needed maybe: to take a deep breath, to let our guards down, to bridge the gap in our relationships a little, and to connect with each other. We had somehow found a beautiful and fun way to muddle through visiting my mom's headstone with her mother and the rest of her immediate family.

By the time we got out of the car, all three of us, but especially my grandmother, were feeling fairly relaxed and jovial. Again, just like weeks before, on that first birthday without my mom, somehow it was an amazing and beautiful experience, all together... in the cemetery. Proving, I suppose, that it is not the location, or the occasion, but rather the company you keep that matters most in any situation. The most memorable part of that adventure... hands down, was the somewhat steep descent down off the hill, from the graveside back to the car. Rather than a sad, somber, grieving mother, there stood an 80-yr-old ball of energy, as she gleefully bounced down the hill with the carefree spirit of a very content child. My Aunt's husband looked at me and said, "I think you broke her... or maybe you fixed her. Either way, she looks pretty content right now." Her son looked at her and asked what was going on with her, to which she giggled, shrugged her shoulders, and whimsically replied to him

, "Lo-ti-do" as she just as carelessly continued about her business, strolling down that hill to get back in the car.

What did she just say?? We all just looked at each other and with no words exchanged, suddenly all just burst into laughter! Walking down from her daughter's grave, surrounded by love and a little encouragement from her new friend, Mary Jane... my grandmother was content for the moment. She got through a seemingly impossible task, and she did it with grace and laughter even. As far as I'm concerned, that entire visit was a giant win and I'm so grateful for that experience! It brought together people who aren't necessarily always on common ground. It helped everyone relax, take a breath and just be present with each other - in memory, and in honor of someone we all loved very much! Without that experience, the bridge may not have been paved for more comfortable and familial future interactions that have occurred since that day. Also, what an amazing story it left us with. That day on the porch with my aunt and my grandmother, we all felt closer to my mom, and to each other. It felt so good to just laugh for the sake of laughing... and to imagine my mom standing there in that circle laughing just as hard as we were!

Permission to Laugh at a Funeral

.

Who Wants Cake

So, what have we learned so far? To quote Michael Franti, "Bad shit happens, but good shit happens too." At that time, added to the list of terrible awful things happening in the world, one of my closest childhood friends had a five-year-old daughter fighting for her life, battling a brain tumor. From an early age, I knew how much I loved helping people by gathering everyone together and doing something fun to raise money for the person(s) in need. So, when a neighbor asked me if I would help plan a fundraiser for our friend, of course I happily agreed! To be honest, I was grateful for the distraction and to seize the opportunity to create a little joy in the middle of everyone's despair.

As it turned out, the fundraiser ended up near my dad's birthday, which set the stage for a perfect birthday surprise for him! We had been looking for something that would boost his spirits and help him remember how loved and adored he really was! Then it hit us! We remembered seeing old photos of our dad who had dressed up and jumped out of a cake for his dad when he retired, many years ago. Our dad would have been around thirty-five at the time and was dressed as a call girl with blackened out teeth, a wig and a bikini - stuffed with balloons, of course.

When trying to come up with fun birthday ideas that would make him smile, recreating some version of that experience was at the top of our list! We asked my paternal grandfather (to flip the script and recreate this for his son), but we never expected him to agree and feed into our nonsense. You could have knocked me over with a feather when he quickly agreed to do it!!! Whatever made him say yes and agree to all the silly details, I am forever grateful for!

My sister and I made a giant cake out of foam poster boards, which stood about 4.5 feet tall. It had to be assembled in different pieces, so that the top could pop right off for the big reveal. With the cake assembled and hidden away until it was time, we were ready for that night to arrive.

First, the fundraiser took place that night, and it was a complete success! It raised a fair amount of money to help the family with the travel and medical expenses. It also brought a large group of people together, united with a common purpose, and raised just as much morale and goodwill as it did money that night! Everyone was overjoyed to be able to give my friend and her daughter back a little bit of the love and joy that they'd created for everyone they've ever met!

Topping off the night, then was our bang-up birthday surprise. Right before turning the rest of the evening over to the DJ, we blindfolded and escorted my dad onto the dance floor. In front of everyone, we sat him down directly in front of his huge birthday cake and then removed his blindfold.

His face, you guys... Remember, his wife had just died. I am very sure in that moment that he thought we had paid a female entertainer to pop out of that cake. His face said it all. It was one of anxiety, embarrassment and complete uncertainty. I'm sure he scanned his brain the entire length of the music playing, wondering who might be inside, while this giant cake just sort of wiggled around in front of him.

Despite giving it some quick but serious thought, I'm not sure he would have even come close to guessing that it was his 80 yr old father!! When the song ended and his moment had arrived, our grandfather, like a complete rockstar, popped the top right off of that cake to reveal himself wearing a beat-up blonde wig and a little black nightie - stuffed with green balloons. As he appeared, he casually threw a handful of confetti, blew a horn and proclaimed, "Happy Birthday!"

My dad's reaction was definitely that of a man who had just witnessed a completely unexpected phenomenon! The pure, unadulterated joy on his face as he clapped and threw his head back in deep belly laughter will always be one of my favorite moments with him. It's such a beautiful thing to see someone just light up in a moment of blissful joy! Dad smiled bigger and laughed harder than maybe I've ever seen him, then he hugged his dad so tightly, green balloons and all, as they continued laughing hysterically together.

We helped our grandfather out of that cake, had a quick family photo shoot, then he changed clothes and came back out to celebrate the rest of the night with his son. My grandfather had taken what could have been a very sad time for his son, and gave him a lighthearted and playful memory instead. Again, collateral beauty that simply would not have existed if not for the devastating events leading up to it. If we can't control the tragedies and traumas that happen to us, at least we can keep searching for and also creating the good, the joy, and the life, in the midst of the chaos and loss.

Permission to Laugh at a Funeral

Permission to Laugh at a Funeral

4PM on Some Idle Tuesday...

One of my favorite songs, or spoken word, is *Everybody's Free (To Wear Sunscreen)* by Baz Luhrmann, adapted from an essay written by Chicago Tribune columnist, Mary Schmich in 1997. Added to the list of **things we must do**, along with 1) Watch *Mickey's Twice Upon a Christmas*, **and** 2) if you ever get a reindeer, name him Murry... **is now** 3) close your eyes and listen to Baz just give you some life advice that's guaranteed to hit you right in the feels. The lines I want to reference now though...

Don't worry about the future
Or worry, but know that worrying
Is as effective as trying to solve an algebra equation
by chewing bubble gum
The real troubles in your life
Are apt to be things that never crossed your worried mind
The kind that blindsides you
at 4 p.m. on some idle Tuesday

Back to that phone call on Christmas day... my grandfather and his declining health had been the focus of our attention at that time, and when my dad called me in a panic, I was convinced that that was going to be the matter at hand. I never expected to open the door that day to a new reality that it was my mom instead who had seemingly vanished out of thin air and would no longer be around. Granted, it was just before 6pm on a Monday in her case, but the sentiment applies. Ironically, if you remember... my thoughts were also consumed that night before with the possibility and fear that for some irrational reason, my own life was ending. As I sat there late Christmas Eve by the light of the tree, I was worried about all kinds of uncertain potential outcomes to current life situations. But my mom's life suddenly, randomly ending... that I can assure you, never crossed my worried mind.

It had now been months since that shocking day, and we were all still muddling through our new normal. Grief was still the epicenter of our world. My husband and I were still living together, although quietly, privately separated and figuring that out more with each passing day. I was working hard to maintain my business and to be a good mom, daughter, sister, friend, etc. Although we were trying to find the joy, life was overwhelming and exhausting. I was hardly the only one feeling that exhaustion, however. For instance, my grandmother was grieving right along with us, tending to her son as much as she could, and at home she was caring for her husband, whose needs were around the clock at this point. My family helped on occasion, and I spent as much time there as I was able to. My grandfather was now in month 9, after it was predicted that he had 6 months to live. He was still declining, though, and he suffered sporadic episodes that became emergent very quickly. He was also, however, relishing every second of quality time left with his wife. That was an honor to watch their connection, knowing it was coming to an end. My parents had the greatest love I have ever witnessed, and they didn't have the chance to say their final goodbyes. In so many ways, though, they didn't need to. They lived an open, say all the things kind of lifestyle and were not shy about how they felt. My grandparents did happen to be awarded the luxury of knowing that their time together would soon end, and they did not intend on wasting one minute of it.

One random summer day my husband and his father showed up at my grandparents' house to help them with their yardwork. I can't remember the day or time, but for conversation's sake… let's just say it was sometime around 4pm on some idle Tuesday. They got out of the car to immediately see my grandfather, unable to go any further because he was tethered to an oxygen tank, yelling for them to come quickly to help his wife. They went running into the house and found her collapsed in the hallway and laying on the floor.

… Blindside.

I knew my grandmother was tired and wearing thin, but I didn't know the extent of her exhaustion. After all, her daughter in law just died, her husband was dying, she was constantly tending to him, she was worried about and grieving alongside her son and his family... how could she not be depleted.

She was completely stubborn sometimes. This was one of those times. They wanted to take her immediately to the hospital, but she refused several times, claiming that she was just tired. Later that night, though, she finally agreed to letting my dad take her to the hospital. I went to stay with her husband. While she was waiting to leave, we sat in her living room together and had an honest conversation. Everyone was sure that she had pneumonia, or some kind of respiratory infection that had her totally run down. She sat in her living room with me and said, "Tosha I don't have pneumonia." I asked, "Does it feel more like bronchitis?" She hesitated and then with complete certainty looked at me and said, "No, I have cancer." I asked her if she knew that for certain or if she was just speculating. She continued, "I don't have to know for sure to know. I can feel it. The pain in my back has been getting worse and I'm getting weaker and more tired."

That night my dad took her to the hospital where her inpatient stay confirmed her worst fears. She did, in fact, have advanced lung cancer. Her body was also pretty frail and not in a strong enough condition to survive the battle of full treatment.

My dad and I were continuously texting back and forth that evening... him from the hospital with his mom, awaiting results from a steady stream of tests, procedures, etc. and me from their home with her husband who was entertaining an impromptu jam session with the neighbors in his living room while trying to work out some nervous, anxious energy at the unknown of his wife being at the hospital. If you recall, playing guitar and rocking out one more time like he did when he was young, was on his bucket list. He did have an epic porch session with the grandson of one of his music icons... but this night was different. This night he was the musician rather than the audience. The neighbors both play guitar as well, and so we ended up with a full on jam session unfolding to distract us from the impending bad news. He drank a few beers, ripped his oxygen off and just went to town playing for hours! My dad and I were texting back and forth comparing notes on our respective evenings, acknowledging that now his mom was dying, and that her husband might be actively dying and experiencing some kind of last burst of energy. There was no other way to explain what was happening with him. He suddenly played with energy and stamina that he hadn't had in years!

Obviously my grandfather hit a wall later that night. I remember watching him go from such joy and excitement to such fear and helplessness. Fortunately, I was able to give him a breathing treatment, calm him down, and get him to sleep peacefully. As it turned out that was not some predeath burst of energy indicating he was actively beginning to die, but rather perhaps, one person's will to throw their anxious energy into something with purpose, and to create the moment he desperately wanted to have again.

With my grandmother in the hospital for a few days, I did have to check my grandfather into respite care - temporarily - because he really did require around-the-clock care. We were able to place him immediately, so I packed him up with the essentials for a couple of days and off we went!

Ugh... you guys! That might be in the top five worst things I have ever had to do in my entire life. It was so sudden. None of us had time to wrap our heads around what was happening or to talk at all about what should or would happen next.

I will never forget wheeling him into the third floor of that building and down a completely empty, drab looking beige hallway. It was the most institutional thing I could have imagined. He was placed in a room at the very end of that long hall, seemingly isolated from the entire world. I felt like a mother leaving her young child at preschool against their will – terrified, unsure, and alone. I tried my best to get him settled in, as much as you could settle in for just a few days. We hugged so tightly, and we just cried a little together. There were so many things happening all at one time. I walked out of that room, walked down that very long, very bleak hallway, walked out of that building and cried hysterically the entire drive home. That. Felt. Unbearable.

This time in my life was definitely the lowest point to date. In the last 12 months: I had found out that my grandfather was dying, had told my husband I wanted a divorce, had suddenly lost my mom, had been grieving while also care giving. I had continued to live with my husband while we figured out separated coparenting life, and had also been trying to run a business, be a mom and still be a person who found joy in her life on top of that pile of shit.

And now... now my grandmother was dying!! My ride or die, my best friend who had become even more important to me after losing my mom, the woman who wasn't afraid to shoot straight with me... now she was dying. The beige hallway was just the final straw, though, having no choice but to drop my grandfather off in the most depressing place I'd ever seen. They say, when it rains it pours... and at this point, building an ark was on the table.

This low point had great purpose, though. It was somewhere around this time that I remember harnessing the power of the Serenity Prayer and making peace with the things that I could not accept. I couldn't control which things in life were going to happen, that was now abundantly clear. I could, however, control how I reacted to them. It was around that time also that I realized that this low point would be the catalyst that prepared me for the next phase of my life.

I had never before felt pain like I was feeling then. I had never truly known torment and anguish until then. I have always been empathetic to and fascinated by the recovery and rebuilding process of people who have experienced trauma, loss and heart ache. It was at that moment that I was able to connect with those emotions on a level that I had never experienced before, and so I began to write about it. I began to keep a timeline of events as they were happening. I would jot down quick notes about events and then also how they made me feel. I didn't have the time or mental capacity then, but I knew that eventually I would put all of those words and thoughts together to be able to tell you all exactly how this time in my life went down, and how learning to understand that we aren't in control of everything but that we can be in control of ourselves in regards to everything, changed my life and made me the version of myself that I am today.

Permission to Laugh at a Funeral

Permission to Laugh at a Funeral

Taking the Power Back

Fortunately, my gram was able to get some rest, fluids and medicine and get home in just a couple of days. By that point, I had received many unhappy, tear-your-heart-out, phone calls from my grandfather, desperately pleading to come home. After just a few days apart, they both returned home, with some very new and different limits imposed, and with the complete awareness that our routines as we had known them were coming to an end. Once they were settled, the three of us sat down and talked about me having power of attorney for both of them and helping guide them through the end of their lives. Completely unsure about what would happen with each of them, we needed to play through all possible scenarios and decide how they really felt about all of the things. We talked about their end of life wishes, their memorial services, what they wanted done with their cremains... we talked about it all. Part of that conversation was facing the reality that I may have to make some hard decisions for them and that they trusted my ability to objectively do that when needed. I remember feeling humbled and incredibly honored that they had asked me to help navigate them through that process.

The first heavy conversation we all had to have was the conversation about transitioning my grandfather to a Veteran's Long Term Care Facility. Despite knowing that the move was inevitable, he first reacted with shock and resistance. I just sat patiently and gently with him on the front porch of his house and let him calm down and slow his breathing. Gently I reminded him that they had both entrusted me with the honor, privilege and responsibility of making difficult decisions with and eventually for them. I brought his awareness to the fact that we had arrived at one of those difficult moments that we needed to figure out together, and that unfortunately it was time to make the difficult decision to move to assisted living. This time though, we had a little more time at our disposal, the ability to do more research and planning, and we had more opportunity to prepare ourselves mentally for it. It happened about a week after gram had come home from that initial hospital visit. In those final days of my grandparents living together, everyone was aware that it was the end of an era and that life was changing in a big way. As a result, we made the most of every minute of that time and we had worked hard to create the best experience we could for both of them in those last days together in their home.

Finally, the day had arrived. My grandfather's room was ready. He was ready. We were ready, or at least as ready as anyone can be when that day comes. This time already felt different, though. To begin with, he had settled into the idea that this was the next phase of his life. Oddly, he was feeling okay. He was even excited about meeting new friends to share war stories and life stories with. My grandmother was facing an influx of appointments and her own uncertainty ahead, as well. The time had come for him to leave, and she had to begin her new journey. He and I drove to the veteran's home, as she was headed to a follow up appointment with her doctor. As we pulled away from their house, after their beautiful, sweet goodbyes, he asked me if I would stop and get him a carton of cigarettes to take with him. I told him that there was absolutely no way that he was taking a carton of cigarettes, but that I would get him one pack and that he was free to smoke them the entire way there if he wanted to.

We pulled into the store for me to go grab his pack of cigarettes, some crossword puzzles, and a few snacks to send with him. I was inside just a minute and came back out to him having pushed every control button in my car. He looked at me like an ornery five-year-old and said, "I think I hit a wrong button." I laughed and asked him what he had been trying to do. He replied that he was trying to put the window down. He had managed to turn on the wipers, the turn signal, the four-way lights, the high beams, the inside light, the AM radio... but god love him, his window was still up. I put his window down, turned everything else off and then we settled in for the drive. He was still on oxygen so when he smoked those cigarettes he so desired, he would reach out the window and hang his oxygen tube from the side mirror. As it blew in the breeze, he held his head slightly out the window, enjoying and embracing what he knew and had accepted as his last real moments of complete freedom in this life.

This time the ride felt so different. This time, we had made the decision. We were in control. There wasn't the same panic or urgency as before. We just took our time driving, looked around, jammed to some of his favorite music, and when we were about twenty minutes away, I told him that there was a packed bowl in the glove box and asked if he had any interest in smoking one last time. You guys... his entire face lit up as he was now dancing and lost in the music in the passenger seat next to me.

He cocked his head, looked at me, and with one hand already on the glove box, replied, "Is that even a question?" He pulled out the hidden surprise and sparked up his last bowl with so much excitement, as Led Zeppelin serenaded us the rest of the way! I remember looking over at him and just thinking about how much joy he was soaking up in those moments. He was living, despite the despair – unapologetically, fearlessly, without a single care in the world.

Admittedly going through the process of placing my grandfather in a home for the second time had given me some hesitancy and reservations, especially knowing that it was for real and forever this time. Still, I was determined and found it pretty easy to be cheerful and optimistic as I helped them both through this time in their lives. After we arrived, I got out of the car to unload the wheelchair and help him. To my surprise, he was standing waiting for me when I got around the car to him. He seemed accepting. He almost even seemed excited, like I was dropping him off at summer camp. We wheeled through the building and followed our directions to find his room. We found it at the exact moment that food service was delivering lunches. They quickly and excitedly asked him his preference from a couple of different options. His face lit up as he chose the lasagna dinner.

We no sooner got him situated and settled when his meal arrived. By this time, it had been about 30 minutes since he had found his surprise in the glove box. So, the timing for all of this, although completely unplanned and by sheer destiny alone, could not have been any better! Basically, at the exact moment the munchies kicked in, he was diving into his salad, lasagna, garlic bread and dessert. He was laughing with the nurses as they all met for the first time. He was smiling. He was accepting this situation like a champion. He was okay. And because he was okay, I was okay. I was able to hug him that afternoon, knowing that he had everything he needed, that he was content, that he had made the most of his situation, and that for just that brief moment... I could drive home with the windows down, get lost in my own music and just catch my own breath for a little while.

The decision had also been made that my grandmother would soon leave to temporarily stay with my uncle and his family, which was a little closer to her doctor appointments. My aunt had been very generous and offered to help care for her in their home and to transport her as needed for her medical needs. If I'm being honest, I really struggled with this at first. I was so close to my grandmother. I had just lost my mom, just dropped my grandfather off, and now she was leaving too. I had been staying with her so much of the time, and even when I wasn't, our houses were only a few minutes apart. Now, she would be a forty-minute drive from my house. I would no longer be able to stop by for quick visits on my way home or just casually check in.

At some point that week after my grandmother came home from the hospital, my dad stopped me as I walked by him and just gently said, "I know you're struggling with this. You've done what you needed to do though for now, let somebody else have a turn. Make peace with it and take a break. It's okay." Whew! That was absolutely what I needed to hear most in the world at that time, even if I didn't know it until that moment.

He was so right though. Not that I could even begin to fully wrap my head around it all in that moment, but I needed some space and time to catch my breath before I headed into the next phase of what was about to happen.

Permission to Laugh at a Funeral

Permission to Laugh at a Funeral

Catching My Breath

...And catch my breath I set out to do. It had been a year at that point, since the conversation when my husband and I had decided that things were over. Although we continued to live together until life settled down, nothing between us had changed. We were still just waiting for things to calm down until we proceeded with any other big life events, like a divorce. We got along fine and continued to share finances and childcare responsibilities. That time spent apart, but living together, made all the difference in allowing us to create this genuine 'best of all worlds' situation that we all thrive in today. I am insanely grateful for the way we decided to play that out. Trust me, it wasn't easy, not even close. There were many hurt feelings and bumps in the road along the way, but we figured out how to talk, how to listen, when to pause, when to respond, and at the end of the day – how to give our daughter the best possible scenario despite the circumstance.

With most of our conflicts resolved, and the most necessary conversations had, I approached the subject of our status with him. It had been a year since we had first made that decision, although life was not getting any less hectic. I remember telling him that I just wanted to clear the air and to make sure that we were still on the same page, reinforcing that nothing had changed for me, despite the fact that we were still living together. He agreed. We were on the same page. He responded by telling me that he assumed we were having that conversation because I was seeing or sleeping with someone. I told him that I wasn't, but that I needed to, if I was being honest. I needed to get out of my head and move on to something new, something that wasn't surrounding me with grief and pain. He amicably accepted what I was telling him... and with that, I felt free to set out to really catch my breath.

The last thing I wanted was a man I was going to see every day. I didn't want a relationship. I didn't want any complications. I really just wanted unattached, temporary, intense human connection – with someone I didn't know and wouldn't see again if I didn't want to. So, with a clear conscience I set out to find exactly what I needed most at that time. With limited to no real free time to actually go out in the world and meet people, I took my search online. I also started to do a lot of soul searching during this time too. Part of that soul searching was me having a conversation with someone I dated and loved many years ago. He is now happily married and I have full respect for that, and for him... but we had always had amazing conversations, and I needed one of those conversations now. I remember him telling me that few men would understand the situation and be comfortable meeting someone who still lived with her husband. I was as clueless as a teenager trying to figure out dating for the first time. I didn't know very much about what I was looking for, but I knew enough to tell him with confidence that the man I needed to find would understand my situation.

Ironically, the day after having that conversation with my friend, I had my first phone conversation with a man I had met online a few days before. He was funny; he was light-hearted; he was a dad who was separated, but because he worked out of town and his separation was relatively new for him, he too still shared a home with his wife. Look at that. I created a clear image of what I wanted and needed at that time, and then I had the confidence to ask for and seek after it, and there we were. I had found someone who not only was tolerant and understanding of my situation, but who also could completely relate to what was happening in my world. He also had a way of having conversations with me that maybe nobody else could have had at that time, as did I for him. We were coming together both from a fragile place, just wanting so badly to restore our faith in the human experience and to create a little healing magic together. I distinctly remember thinking that he was like this reflection of my inner psyche, who had this ability to gently and kindly, but firmly and with conviction, reflect back to me the things I most needed to hear at that time.

After a week or so of talking on the phone, he asked if I wanted to meet for dinner. Don't get me wrong, in my early twenties I was no stranger to the random beauty of meeting and sharing experiences with people I had just met... however, a lot of life had happened since my last random adventure. Now I had a daughter to consider. Also, I hadn't been with anyone new in over a decade, and dating is terrifying sometimes, let's be honest. As much as I wanted to let myself just be free and go meet this man, I couldn't seem to get past the irrational yet overwhelming fear that with absolute certainty he was going to kill me and that my daughter would never see her mom again.

One afternoon as we were texting about it, I joked with him about not wanting to wake up missing a kidney or missing entirely. Immediately my phone rang, and it became our first facetime. Suddenly any confidence and charisma I had completely disappeared. I was talking a big game behind the security of my keyboard, but now I was about to speak face to face with this man. I nervously answered the phone and there he was on the screen – kind, smiling, and completely adorable. He said to me, "Hi, I'm just calling quick to show you that I'm just a guy, at work, trying to make plans with a cute girl. I just wanted you to see my face and to tell you that I have no interest in cutting out your kidney or harming you. If anything, I have a bad knee and could use a new one of those."

I'm not gonna lie, that call definitely helped take the edge off. We only talked for a few minutes, but we followed up later that night with our first of many much longer conversations about any and all of the things. As we talked about life and got to know each other a little more, I realized that he was just a guy who works all day and comes home to chill out and hit the reset. I was much less afraid after that, that he was going to cut out an organ if we ever decided to meet.

After spending a little while getting to know each other on facetime, I was comfortable enough to meet him. Or at least after a pep talk from my girlfriends I was. I also had a conversation with myself in the mirror and made the conscious decision to do this for me. I needed to connect with this man, and lord knows I deserved to take the time for myself, in the middle of such deep grief, with more loss on the horizon.

That next Sunday afternoon I made the two-hour trip to go and have that adventure. Most of the drive I spent getting lost in music; but about half an hour before I arrived, I found myself suddenly really missing my mom. I imagined how much she would have loved to hear about a crazy adventure like that. Unable to call my mom, I decided to call my aunt and tell her instead. Until this point, nobody except a friend or two knew what I was doing or even that I was entertaining the idea of meeting someone.

My aunt answered the phone and asked, "What's up sweetie?" I told her "I'm just driving to Harrisburg and I have a story that my mom would have loved, but because I can't tell her, I wanted to tell you." She began to ask before interrupting herself, "What are you doing in... Oh, wait, you're meeting that guy!"

Hang on a minute... I was in fact, headed to meet this guy, but she wasn't aware of said guy, or even that the idea of him existed. Instantly I began to wonder all kinds of strange things – What did her husband do for a living again? Did they have some weird surveillance on us to make sure we were okay after mom died? All irrational thoughts, but how did she know what I was doing?

I replied to her, "Actually... I am going to see a guy, but how do you know that?" She said, "I don't know. The guy with the dogs, right?" What?? I didn't know much about him yet, but he did have two dogs that he loved almost as much as his son. I just said, "What in the world? For real, how do you know that?" She sort of laughed and just said, "Your mom told me." "Okay, follow up question... Mom has been gone for ten months, how is that possible?" I challenged back. She said, "Well obviously not now, but like two years ago she told me about him. He has a kid, right?" WHAT IN THE ACTUAL HELL??? I reminded her that two years ago I had been very married and absolutely not looking to date. What she said next, I could never have seen coming, even in the middle of the weird that was already happening. She just said, "Tosha I don't know… His name is Daniel, right?"

I give up!! You guys… she knew that I was going to Harrisburg to see a man… she knew that he had dogs… and a kid… and that his name was Daniel!!! Make any of that make sense! For the record, I had never dated anyone from Harrisburg - it's a few hours from my home. I had never dated anyone with dogs, ever actually. And the only man I have ever dated who had a child, I married. I had never dated anyone named Daniel, or anything resembling it. When I tell you there was no rational explanation for my aunt knowing what she knew, I mean just that. All she could offer, as if it was totally normal, was, "I don't know how I know, Tosha… All I can say is that I can plainly hear your mom's voice telling me about him." At this point in our conversation, as I sat in complete disbelief, I told her that I was pulling into the restaurant where I was meeting him and that he was already standing there waiting. She told me she loved me; we laughed; and I hung up the phone.

I got out of the car, and he greeted me with the warmest, most genuine embrace. Now that this beautiful man stood in front of me, I realized that he was the embodiment of every characteristic that I would have selected if I were custom making him for me in that moment. I just held onto him for a minute, and then as we walked into the restaurant, I broke the ice by saying, "So, I just called to tell my aunt about you… and as it turns out, she already knew because,

well, my dead mom had already told her all about you."
As he opened the door, he turned to look at me,
surprised and confused. I just laughed and said, "Sorry
for the shock value, but that's how I'm feeling right
now, and I just needed us to be on the same page so we
can talk about it." To say the least, that definitely broke
the ice and opened the door for lots of interesting
conversation over dinner.

We had a great time at dinner, especially given that
it was each of our first dates in over a decade. It was
relaxed and friendly. I felt the instant familiarity of a
lifelong friendship, and the excitement of a new one...
one where we could be uninhibited, free to be our most
authentic selves during that paused, deliberate
moment in time. As we laughed together like old
friends, we became more and more comfortable with
each other. The connection was just perfect for what
we both needed it to be. As for the rest of that night...
well, let's just say that the details from the rest of that
night make for an incredible story all on their own... but
we'll save that one for another time.

I will say this... that night, that man... was every
single thing that I needed him to be. It was fun. It was
carefree. It was simple. Two human beings who
needed to pause time and create a beautiful safe space
together to catch their breath, came together and did
just that. We laughed. We talked. We played. We hit
the reset button for each other.

We hit that reset button about six or seven times that night actually, just for good measure.

The next morning was an early one for both of us. Having really only napped quickly, we headed back to our own realities just after sunrise that morning. He walked me to my car, hugged me goodbye and kissed me on my cheek. Then as he continued to hold me close, he whispered softly into my ear… "And I'm sending you home with both kidneys." It was the perfect banter to end with. What a fantastic night! I drove the two hours home in that early morning sunshine with a renewed outlook and an incredible amount of new energy.

As great as that night was though, we need to circle back to my aunt who seemed to know every detail of my plans, despite me never having told her or anyone in my family. After I took some time driving that morning to just listen to music, admire my crazy hair & giant smile in the mirror, and get my head straight, I called her from the road. She answered, "Good morning, sweetie… are you okay? How was your night?" I almost couldn't even speak as I just burst out in giggles, then managed to respond, "My night was fantastic. Top notch. Every single thing that I needed it to be." We laughed together and I told her the dirty details of the night and all the silly crazy parts to our adventure. And then I said, "But okay… we need to circle back to how the hell you knew what I was doing last night." She got quiet, dead serious and answered, "Tosha… I don't know what to tell you. When I hung up the phone, my husband looked at me and said – okay, but how did you know all of those things – and I just stared blankly at him. All I could tell him was that I could hear your mom telling me all about him as plain as day. I don't know when or how, but I can remember hearing her tell me."

Driving home that day, feeling so deliciously at peace, I actually didn't need to question or explain it all any further. Here's what I did know... I knew that this man seemed to be specifically chosen, down to the very last detail for me, for what we both had needed from life in that moment. I am so certain that my mom did tell my aunt somehow, that if I were able to talk to her today, all these years later, that would still be the first thing I would ask her. I would simply smile, wink, and say, "Hey... about Daniel, you did that right?" Knowing full well, especially after hearing it from my aunt, that meeting him was nothing short of a beautiful act of literal divine intervention. To wrap up our phone conversation, my aunt concluded with... "Tosha, as if that bathroom mirror that night wasn't freaky enough, there's no way after this that I can dress as your mom for Halloween!" Ha! Ha! Ha! We burst out laughing, and with that our hopes of morbid, dark, Halloween pranks were really put to rest.

Daniel and I continued to talk and support each other through our respective situations, but we knew that our connection existed as nothing more than a beautiful, honest, weird and wonderful friendship where we would duck in and out of each other's lives from time to time. He was so incredibly helpful during this time,though, and I will never be able to begin to thank him enough. I am very proud to still call him a friend all these years later. Again, a bright spot that came only from a very dark time. Collateral beauty is everywhere!

Permission to Laugh at a Funeral

What Happens Now...

After the drive home that morning, I got a shower and then went to pick my grandmother up so she could visit with her husband before she moved in with my aunt and uncle for the interim to begin her treatments. Gram was one of my best friends, so driving with her that day – taking her to visit the man in her life, telling her about the man in my life from last night – it just felt carefree, juvenile, and fun for a moment. It was nice to be light-hearted for a little while, despite the heaviness of our reality; a heaviness that became very real on our drive home.

My grandparents had a pretty good visit. Mentally and physically he was feeling great, much better than she was at that time. This time, it was Gram who I was pushing in the wheelchair down the hall to his room. We all talked and laughed together, retelling old stories and laughing like we used to; then I took a little walk and gave them some time to be alone.

As we went to leave, she became quite somber and just hugged him so tightly. She looked up at him so sincerely and gently said, "This is gonna be the last time we ever see each other." She kissed him and just held on to him so tightly. He calmed her and tried to assure her that it definitely would not be. She just smiled softly with her eyes low and nodded slightly as she sat back down.

Whew! The major life moments were stacking up! Now that I was able to breathe again, I had a quiet moment of reflection with myself and remember very distinctly coming to a place of not only acknowledgement, but also a place of gratitude. I didn't spiral in anger, which would have been perfectly acceptable given the mounting stress and loss. I rather found myself soaking up every single precious moment, with the full realization that my time with some of my very favorite people was quickly coming to an end, and the acute awareness that life is fragile and completely unpredictable. I had the rare opportunity to embrace life fully, even and especially in those moments, and to enjoy them for exactly what they were - bittersweet, beautiful, major life moments. Every doctor appointment with one of them, every difficult conversation, every heartfelt breakdown in fear of the inevitable – I was incredibly aware in each of those moments that it was truly an honor and a privilege to be able to be present and to help guide them through that time.

At first I resisted the idea of having my grandmother move in with my aunt and uncle, because I selfishly wanted to be with her every day. I knew that she was leaving. I knew that her time with us was ending. My dad's voice just echoed through my mind telling me that it was okay to release the need for that control, to just breathe and to let someone else have a turn.

And so I did. I began to find joy watching her connect more deeply with everyone throughout her final months, knowing that we were so closely connected already. I had peace with my mom's death, largely because we were so closely connected and there were no stones left unturned. With that sentiment in mind, it felt great to watch my grandmother connect with everyone in her world and to have the chance to wrap up her life so eloquently, even in the midst of a devastating disease and her own grief.

Having everyone involved also created opportunities for conversations where we could share our thoughts and make sure that we were all on the same page. This was an incredible human experience for me too, and a life lesson in solid adult communication. One day my dad, my uncle and I were sitting on the porch talking. It was clear that we had conflicting viewpoints and opinions on some matters. I remember just taking a breath and realizing as I sat with them that they were about to lose their mother. I could empathize so much in that moment and I understood that everything driving their words and actions was derived entirely from the place of a son about to lose his mother.

As we sat in silence for a moment and took a collective breath, I told them that we would all be fine and that we would get through this together as long as we were tolerant of each other's differences and calmly searched for the middle ground. For example, my uncle had no interest in the home hospice experience, should we find ourselves at that point. That is not a way that he wanted to remember his mother, and he was adamant that he would not sit bedside as she died. As he released that he absolutely didn't want to, and received back that he absolutely didn't have to, (and that there was nothing wrong with that at all) the air seemed to lighten a little. I shared that as much as he didn't want to do that, I couldn't imagine not being right beside my grandmother when the time came, and that I was looking forward to the opportunity to share her final moments with her.

Releasing him from the pressure he felt at the thought of doing something he desperately didn't want to do, freed him up to jump in and say, "But I don't mind supporting the mission. I'm just not doing the home healthcare end of things." And he brilliantly went on to do just that. Everyone seemed to have their specific roles in the equation and when honest communication was added to it, the system just seemed to work really well. For the next month or so my gram lived with them, and my aunt was amazing as she became the primary point of contact for all things medical for her.

With my grandfather settled into the Veteran's Home and my grandmother settled in with my aunt and uncle, I was free to check back into the rest of my reality a little more than I had been. At home there was a kindergartner and an 8th grader – both beautiful, smart, athletic girls who had a lot happening in their worlds too, meanwhile none of that stopped while other parts of my world were spinning out of control. A million kudos to their daddy for picking up all of the slack during that time!! The girls were just fine; life was moving along nicely for them. For the most part, they were relatively unaffected by most of it. He was holding down the fort like a champion!

My massage therapy business is another area of my life that I hadn't had a lot of time or energy to invest in during that time. My clients, though, could not have been more understanding and supportive, not only as someone providing a service for them, but also as a friend. They rolled with the punches and allowed me the courtesy of shifting appointments when needed. One or two kind souls even tolerated having to let themselves out of the office if I had to rush out in the middle of a session due to an emergency. I love my job, genuinely so much, and I feel incredibly fortunate to be able to say that and really mean it. I pour my heart and soul into the work that I do and I think that people can feel that, which made it easy for them to respond with kindness and understanding when I was quite sincerely unavailable, either physically or mentally for them. Their generosity and patience will never be forgotten or lost on me! One beautiful ray of sunshine even gifted me what she called a "Sunshine Box" which was filled with a cute plant, bright yellow tissue paper and so many beautiful bright happy treats! That gesture was so special to me because the box, combined with the smile on her face when giving it to me, actually did assure me that brighter days were ahead!

Permission to Laugh at a Funeral

Permission to Laugh at a Funeral

Home Sweet Home

A month or so later, the treatments had really begun to start having an effect on my grandmother. Radiation therapy had done some damage to her esophagus, and she complained of what felt like to her, a constant painful lump in her chest as well as pain in her back. She was not physically strong enough to consider chemotherapy at that time. The goal was to build up her strength first, giving her a chance to fight the cancer. Her sadness at the thought of losing her husband, accompanied by the chronic pain she was feeling, and the weak physical state of her body, made it very difficult for her to reach that goal, however. She did not seem to be progressing at all, but rather seemed to be getting weaker and more fatigued by the day.

She was very well cared for and had quite a lavish and comfy set-up, having taken over the basement level of my uncle's home. Sometime in mid-November, though, she had the weekend free from treatments and wanted to stay in her own home for a few days. I agreed to care for her there and was excited to have that time with her. As soon as she arrived home and settled in, I immediately knew that she was not okay. It had been a week or so since I had last seen her, and now she just seemed so frail. Just the forty-minute drive that day completely exhausted her. Later that evening, lying in bed, she suddenly became nauseous. Too weak to get out of bed, she could only manage the strength to lean her head over the bed, throwing up all over the floor beside her bed. She was mortified that I had to clean her vomit, but scrubbing that floor next to her bed that night was something I was so glad to have the opportunity to do. I told her that I was happy to care for her and that it felt good to give back to her some of the unconditional love that she had given me for so many years. When I was young, she used to tease me about how I would inevitably spill my chocolate milk every time I visited her house. We laughed as we reminisced and then I reassured her that it was just my turn to clean up after her now. She settled back onto her pillow, took a quiet moment, smiled, and seemed contented at that response.

At some point the next day I washed her hair for her, and we let my five-year-old style it. She, of course, wanted to give her gram a mohawk. After a minute, though, it became clear that it wasn't as much fun for my gram as it was for Stella. Now visibly uncomfortable, she asked if I would just style her hair like normal. And listen, I would have been happy to oblige her. I could tell she needed to rest, and I wanted to quickly help her... but in that moment, having been face to face with this woman on a regular basis for over thirty years... I could not tell you for a million dollars how she styled her hair. It's short and so I didn't think there were that many options. Still, I couldn't figure it out. I tried parting her hair down the middle, which resulted in her looking exactly like one of the Three Stooges. A nice part on either side wasn't working either. She just kept saying, "Just part it how I usually do, Tosha!" Despite knowing that she was not feeling well and that she was more than frustrated, all I could do was laugh and tell her that apparently, I had no idea how she parted her hair. She finally took the comb, asked me to hold the mirror and parted it with the first inch or so forward for some kind of bang effect, and the rest she combed entirely back! Horizontal, not vertical part! Who knew?!

Later that night I put my daughter to bed in another room and laid down next to my gram in bed. She held my hand and told me that she was running out of energy and that she was a little fearful and uncertain of it all. Such sweet, tender moments where the roles were reversed. I now had the honor of caring for and comforting her, just as she had for me my entire life. I had learned that sense of caring from my dad, I suppose, who had always been a natural caregiver. As a young teen, I watched him care for his aunt through the very long and traumatic end of her life. He handled all of it with such compassion and grace and most importantly, he taught me that you don't have to know how, you just have to want to show up and figure it out. This felt like my time to do that same thing for my gram, and despite it simultaneously breaking my heart, it also gave me a strong sense of peace and calm. As she laid next to me, telling me that she was getting tired, I just told her that not a single one of us wanted to see her go, but that it was absolutely okay if her time here was ending. That moment really brought life full circle for us, as it could not have been any more reminiscent of our conversation years prior when I had talked to her about giving her sister permission to let go and to be done whenever she was ready. Our experience when her sister was dying where I was able to help give my grandmother the strength to face that reality with her sister, now made it very comfortable and natural for us to be so candid with each other as my grandmother's life was coming to an end.

The plan was for gram to return to my uncle's house on Sunday, but when Sunday came, I couldn't convince her to even get out of bed for me to take her. After many phone calls back and forth and much deliberation with my family, we decided that it was best for me to take her to the hospital rather than to their house. At this point, her walking the ten steps to the bathroom was almost impossible. It took me several hours and a lot of coaxing to get her into my car to head to the hospital. My aunt met us at the hospital, as she had all of Gram's recent and updated medical information. The ER was efficient and as fast as they could be, nevertheless, we were still there for a few hours. Some things just happen for reasons you can't explain at the time, but that have incredible, divine purpose. For me, the three of us in that ER exam room that night was one of those things. None of us can be counted on to be very serious in any situation, but when together in that moment, trying to make light of what was happening... well, it was the silly breath of fresh air that we all needed in that moment. Possible projected outcomes didn't matter that night, just the precious, hilarious moments being made in the meantime.

Gram was admitted that night. The scans showed that her lungs were very congested, and simply breathing for her at this point was very difficult. The next morning, the doctor performed a procedure to open her airway and also to insert a feeding tube to try and build her strength back up. The hospital was very honest with us and prepared us for the possibility that she may not survive the surgery. It would give her some temporary relief if it did, but there were absolutely no guarantees given her current condition. We all said our goodbyes to her in the hallway, and then the nurses (with tears in their eyes) wheeled her away. In that moment, we were all unsure as to whether we would get to embrace her ever again. Thankfully, she came out of surgery fine, and they were able to successfully complete both of their intended procedures. Simultaneously, our family was getting to spend some amazing quality time together; even if it was in uncomfortable vinyl chairs with *The Price is Right* playing in the background. We were embracing life in the middle of death. We were finding joy in the middle of sorrow. We were giving ourselves permission to laugh in the middle of heartache, even if it was in a quiet, or not so quiet, waiting room in a hospital.

Gram continued her stay in the hospital, in an effort to regain some strength. At some point that following week, though, my dad and aunt & uncle met with the doctor for an update on her status. When my dad got home, he was all worked up and beside himself. It had been eleven months since he had suddenly and traumatically watched his wife die as she sat next to him in their living room. He was coming up on that anniversary and was now trying to wrap his head around losing his mom too. In agitation and desperate fear, he said to me, "The doctor estimated that she has about a month to live! It's gonna happen at Christmas. I fucking know it is!!!"

I just sat there calmly and then replied, "So?" He whipped his head around so fast and looked at me with giant eyes like what the hell?!? I continued... "So... So what? We've already been through that. You think that losing someone on December 25th is the most terrible thing, but I'm willing to bet that Tuesday, July 15th would feel just as awful." His face softened slightly at the realization that we had already made it through this horrific reality once. Then I said, "Also, bright side... if she dies close enough to Christmas we can have the 2nd Annual Mills Family Ugly Christmas Sweater Funeral." His face!!! He burst into laughter and finally took a breath. Remember, we can't always control *the what* that is happening to us, but we can always control the *way we respond* to it.

It was also around this time that I had asked my dad if one of our family friends was at my mom's viewing or if we had just talked to him sometime afterwards. It's so hard to remember all of the details from those days. My words to him precisely though, were "Hey, do you remember if he was at mom's party or if we just ran into him after it somewhere?" Dad tilted his head, raised his eyebrows and said, "I don't know, Tosha… but did you just call your mom's funeral a party??"

Hmm…. I suppose I had. I laughed and said, "Well wasn't that the point? Didn't we want it to feel like one last party with Bonita and a genuine joyful celebration of her life?!" How interesting to have just casually said it like that, though… and to honestly mean that even today. Looking back on it, it does actually feel like a party… and she would have loved it!

Permission to Laugh at a Funeral

The Beginning of the End

Gram remained in the hospital for the next two weeks. Late Wednesday evening, the night before Thanksgiving, after a very brief feeding tube tutorial she was discharged, and my aunt & uncle were instructed to take her home. In my opinion, she should never have been discharged in her condition.

They had an unimaginable time with her in their home, as almost every single movement that she made would cause her to shriek in pain and to seize up completely. They stuck it out as long as they could but it wasn't long before they had to call for an ambulance to get her back to the hospital.

Over the weekend her condition did not change. She was stable but still declining. Tuesday evening I got a call from the hospital looking for my grandmother. I explained that she was on the 11th floor, surprised that they didn't know that. They explained they were calling from Outpatient Surgery regarding her procedure scheduled for the next day. I explained that the appointment they were referring to had been scheduled before she was admitted and that she absolutely wouldn't be strong enough to survive any surgery now. They agreed and apologized for the confusion. They were equally aware and agreeable that surgery would not be happening, in light of new information they had just been given.

To be completely sure, however, I ended that call and immediately called the nurse's station on the 11th floor. I explained that Outpatient Surgery had just called and that my grandmother, under no circumstances, would be having surgery tomorrow. They agreed that it was absurd and assured me that it would not be happening, as it was simply an oversight. I went to bed thinking that the problem had been a simple one and that it had been quickly resolved.

I woke up to a different reality. My dad called the hospital early that morning to find out how her night had been. The response he received was, "Oh, she's doing well. She's just coming back now from her surgery. Looks like everything went well." What in the world?! The surgery that, on the phone the night before, I had made very clear would not be happening and was assured and reassured would not be happening had, in fact, just happened without any of us present or even aware of it. For the time being, though, I chose to hang on more to the "she's doing well" part and less to the "coming back from surgery" part.

When the girls got out of school that afternoon, we drove straight to the hospital. Gram was in a complete state of deep sleep, not aware that any of us were even in the vicinity. I sat there and just looked at her. You can know that the end is coming, but having your loved one now unable to communicate with you is a whole new level of painful realization.

At some point I met with the doctor who paced nervously back and forth outside the room before coming in. She began the conversation by telling me that my grandmother had suffered a cardiac episode... "following her procedure," of course. Now this woman was understandably sweating a little at having to tell me that news. Following a surgery that was unauthorized and that had actually been clearly instructed not to happen, gram's status had now changed drastically. Although she was stable, she just laid there in that state of deep sleep. After about the third or fourth overcompensating time that the doctor entered the room to express her sympathy and to ask if I needed anything I finally just stood up, looked at her and was very honest. I said, "Look, we both know you guys messed this one up. Luckily for you I have had my share of pain recently and I have no interest in creating more for anyone else. But please, go anywhere else right now before I change my mind."

The girls and I sat at her bedside for a while that afternoon, along with my dad's sister. Gram was not coherent or awake for even one minute of the time we were there that evening. I left the hospital that night

189

knowing that I had to begin to make peace with the fact that she was approaching the end of her life.

Thursday I took the girls to school and decided that I couldn't and honestly didn't want to do anything else except go and sit with her. I also wanted to be there when the doctors all made their rounds that day. We needed to get on the same page and talk about what was happening with her now and what needed to happen next.

When I walked into her room that morning, she was the same as the day before. She was sleeping, unaware that I was even present. Eventually, though, different from the day before, she woke up suddenly and reached for me. That was promising. A little glimmer of encouragement in the middle of such uncertainty. I went right to her side. She just grabbed me and squeezed me so tightly. I mean, so tightly. The kind of hug that you remember and cherish forever. The one like my mom had given me on her porch that night we all last spent time together with her sister.

Gram looked at me with this childlike wonder and overwhelming joy that I'll never forget. She said, "Oh, Tosha... isn't it just beautiful?!" as she looked up and toward the top corner of her room. I put my face next to hers and I said "Tell me what you see." She continued staring on with such peaceful, beautiful amazement as she continued, "...All of the people! All of the people just waiting to see me. Isn't it so beautiful?!"

Now... I should pause to tell you that while my mom never shared her religious views with me because she didn't feel like they were similar to mine and she respected that, my gram and I had very similar views on spirituality and the world at large, and we talked about it fairly often. I can tell you with absolute certainty that while my mom may have been predisposed to imagine a group of people waiting to greet her upon her death, my Gram did not subscribe to that thought process and would never have been expecting to see that image. What she was describing to me, though, could not have been more genuine and the emotion behind it was just as real.

She spent most of that day fading in and out of deep sleep where she either had no awareness that I was even in the room, or she was suddenly awake and overjoyed to see me, wanting to soak up every single ounce of love and togetherness she could get her hands on. At one point she woke up and sat up with her arms extended to hug me again. This time when I went to hug her, she knocked my hat off with her fiery little demeanor, telling me that she could get a better hug without it on. And then just as quickly, she settled back onto the bed and drifted to sleep again. It was like a bittersweet game we were playing.

I took the opportunity to have real and candid conversations with the doctors that day. Prior to this incident, we were being told that she was still being considered for transfer to a rehab facility. That day we came to the obvious conclusion that she wouldn't be able to complete the physical work necessary to qualify for rehab, especially now that she was not even awake. The doctor started the conversation by talking around the subject, which was appreciated, however I quickly told them that I was in a place where I was quite familiar and comfortable with the awful inevitable truth that her time was coming to an end. We then were able to have a real conversation and decided that it was time to have our family meet to discuss what was about to happen in her world.

We all met at the hospital early the next morning to be to meet with the doctor. When I walked into her room that morning, my dad's siblings were already there, and gram was sitting up in bed talking and laughing with them like she would have a year prior. Imagine my disbelief when I walked into that room. I knew, though, that one of two things was happening. Either she had been on a fair amount of painkillers the days prior and was coming back to life a little, or the more obvious – she really was about to leave us, and this was her big rally before she checked out.

We all met with the doctor in a private waiting room – my dad, my aunt and her husband, my uncle... all of us. This was a weird one for me.. I had been entrusted with the responsibility of helping guide her logistically through the end of her life, and I was more than prepared to do that. However, now I was sitting in a room with all of her children and wanted to be extremely cautious not to step on any toes or to upset anyone who might have wanted to help her with those same things. As we waited for the doctor, we all had one of those genuine honest conversations, similar to the one that my dad and my uncle and I had on the porch weeks prior. As we sat there waiting for the doctor to tell us what happens next, we all found ourselves very able to just be honest and accept where we all were at. We worked together to devise a home hospice plan where everybody would get what they needed and wanted from the situation, but more importantly, one where nobody had to be in a situation they didn't want to be in.

I did more listening than talking in that room at first and was studying how my family all seemed to really feel and be doing. My aunt seemed sad and overwhelmed. She did not seem to have any interest in being the assertive voice in the crowd. My dad, who had taken this role so naturally before, was broken himself and still trying to find his way back to the surface. He had no capacity for handling this situation. That left my uncle, who had been our rock when my mom died. He did not have the same energy now. This time, he was the one losing his mom. It was my turn to help them and carry some of this burden. I also felt prepared, harnessing a strength and insight that I didn't have before and had only recently developed out of necessity.

After the doctor came in, I asked one question before we would decide how to proceed. We needed to know for sure what was happening with her that day. I asked about the history of the pain meds issued during the two days prior so that we could determine if she had just been highly medicated, making her incoherent. The doctor agreed it was a valid point and looked back through her chart to discover that her last pain medicine had been issued at 4am Thursday morning. I had been present for that next dose scheduled and I had told them to hold off because she was sleeping well and hadn't shown any signs of discomfort. It was now Friday morning. The doctor confirmed that gram's actions the previous day were not the side effects of narcotics but had been, in fact, her actual experiences as they were happening to her. Gram was likely experiencing her rally phase, which made her so full of life for the time being. She really was preparing to leave us.

As we discussed our options, the doctor told us that we had the choice to have that same procedure done to open her lungs again but that we were just continuing the cycle, and that most likely she would not survive it a third time. Aside from making that choice, the doctor told us that we were at the point of maintaining comfort measures only and that they would be doing their best to make the end of her life as enjoyable as possible. The doctor talked to us about possibly having her transferred to the 14th floor, which was the terminal unit. We all kind of laughed and my uncle stated that there was no way she would agree to that. She had been very vocal about the 14th floor and having siblings who died on there. We continued our family conversation as we explored all of our options, decided to take her home on hospice, then talked about where everyone stood on that - emotionally, logistically, and practically. After some amazing honest conversation we had a pretty solid plan in place that worked for everyone.

The doctor then asked how we wanted to tell gram. She asked who, if any of us, would be included or did we want the doctor to talk to her privately about it. I was fighting the urge to jump up and scream that I wanted to be the one to do it. I couldn't imagine not being beside her when she got that news, but I also didn't want to impose myself over her own kids who should have that right if they wanted it. We all sat in silence for a minute trying to process everything. Finally, my uncle broke the silence and said, "I think Tosha should be in there with her. They have some weird connection and she has a way of making her listen to her." My heart burst in that moment. We were all on the same page. It was a devastating book we were reading, but we were all on the same page. I took a deep breath and just looked at them and smiled softly.

The doctor and I left the waiting room and walked together to gram's room. As we walked, I carefully searched for the right words as I prepared for what I was going to say to her. Gram was still all smiles and so happy that this seemed like confusing and unnatural news to be giving her. The doctor sat on one side of her bed and I sat on the other. The doctor had told me on our walk to her room that she (the doctor) would take my lead and jump in as much as I needed her to, but that she understood and could sense that I wanted to be the one to tell her. She started the conversation by asking my Gram up until what point did she want to continue fighting this disease. My gram looked at her with the hopeful eyes of an excited toddler and replied, "I want to fight until there's nothing more that can be done." The doctor looked at me. I smiled softly as I took a deep breath, letting her know I was ready to speak. I took my grandmother's hand and remember telling her, "We are at that point now. Everything that can be done has been done." She just looked at us with the absolute sincerity and vulnerability of a child and calmly just responded, "Okay." The doctor chimed in that she needed to tell her how beautiful and amazing our family seemed to be handling this. At that point I started to cry. Immediately my Gram grabbed my hand and said, "That's enough of that... there don't need to be tears. I am okay." Too late for that, the flood gates had already been opened. The doctor and I sat there on opposites sides of her bed as we both held one of my grandmother's hands and sat around her bed soaking in that moment. I told them, though, that I wasn't crying because she was dying. I was genuinely moved at how our family was responding to it also, and having the doctor acknowledge it just made it wash over me. We just sat there for a few minutes and talked about the collateral beauty of life, somehow walking away from that experience feeling lighter and freer than I could have ever imagined in that situation.

During that conversation, we also talked about options with her and how she wanted to handle everything now that it had become real. Gram reinforced and made it abundantly clear that she wanted to be home when she passed. We had also presented her with the option of "transferring to a different part of the hospital that would be more comfortable" Exactly as predicted, as the words were still coming out of the doctor's mouth, gram shot up and demanded that she wasn't going to the damn 14th floor. It was out of the question!

The doctor and I walked back to the waiting room with my family and the doctor told them that I had handled that conversation with elegance and admirable strength. I'm not sure why, but that compliment meant more to me than most accolades I have received in this lifetime. She also told them that we tried skirting around the floor number and that she had a strong reaction in opposition to being moved to another location – unless that location was home, which she was anxious to do.

Since this meeting took place on Friday morning. we decided we would use the weekend to get organized and prepare her house to bring her home on Monday after everything was ready and hospice care was put in place. Having talked through the logistics, and with a solid plan agreed upon, we walked back over to enjoy the day of full energy with gram and to soak in as much quality time as we could!

Although she was alert and full of energy that day, she also wasn't making a whole lot of sense and was experiencing hallucinations that the rest of us weren't privileged to. One glimpse of the ridiculous humor that came from that day happened when Bill from Outpatient Surgery strolled into the room whistling, holding his clipboard that held a consent for yet another surgical procedure. With the ferocity of a mother lion, I turned to him and asked what he thought he was doing. I took the opportunity to introduce myself as her power of attorney and the person who would be signing off on anything, certainly not her. Bill from outpatient surgery had been the direct link to setting Wednesday's unauthorized and highly objected procedure into motion. He snipped back at me and told me that she seemed perfectly fine to sign her own documents. Again, with eyes that could kill, I snidely asked him to have her explain who Sue was, as I motioned to the white board and empty chair at the foot of the bed. He looked back at me perplexed. I snapped back, "Exactly… I don't see her either. Yet five minutes ago I was scolded for being rude and not giving Sue my chair when, God love her, she's been standing all day." I reminded Bill about the unauthorized procedure from two days prior and told him that she was now in the system as comfort measures only and that quite simply, he needed to keep moving and find anything else to do.

Permission to Laugh at a Funeral

Permission to Laugh at a Funeral

It Takes a Village

I went home Friday night, not wanting to leave her, but needing to spend some time and energy getting everything in my day-to-day life prepared for me to step away from it for a short time. Finally, early Saturday evening I had gotten to a place where I could step away. I drove to visit and spend some time with her, stopping first at my grandfather's to check in with him. His health was continuing to decline, but he was still doing okay. He and I sat and had an honest, candid conversation about what was happening with gram and that she would be going home to spend her final days. He became obviously distraught but handled the news fairly well, all things considered. Once he had calmed down and was back in a place of rest, I continued on to see Gram.

When I got to the hospital, she was awake and semi-alert. She grabbed my arm, and I mean gripped me tightly… and said, "Tosha… get me the fuck out of here." I looked at her, surprised and then kind of laughed. I asked, "Are you alright?" She told me, "I do not want to die in the hospital. Get me home now!" I very softly but seriously looked at her and asked, "Do you think you're dying today?" She replied, "I don't know, but I know it's not going to be long, and I want to be home." I smiled reassuringly and told her that I would handle it. I went out to the nurses' station and asked about contacting a hospice nurse now rather than waiting until the next day. She told me that the woman we needed was still at the hospital and that she had the paperwork already drawn up for us. As I began calling her kids to get everyone on the same page, my dad and his cousin walked off the elevator. His sister was on her way also to check in on her mom. I pulled him aside and quickly explained what had just happened and that she was set on going home that night. I told him that I had offered to stay with her overnight at the hospital, but she insisted that we get her home.

We called my uncle who left his house for hers immediately to start moving some things around to prepare a space for the hospital bed. My dad and I had a conversation with the hospice representative at the hospital and he and his cousin, as well as his sister who had just arrived were planning to stay with gram until she left in an ambulance to return home. I kissed her goodbye and then left to meet my uncle to help get things ready at her house. My dad was understandably feeling anxious and unprepared at walking off the elevator into a suddenly new and scary reality. I remember him telling the nurse that we hadn't even learned how to use the feeding tube yet and I just quietly said to him, "Dad... we aren't taking the feeding tube home with us." The nurse agreed and gently explained to him that her body no longer needed or required more food. It had enough reserve that she would not starve, and that she wasn't going to feel hungry during those final days. That act of digesting food right now would cause irritation and take a great deal of energy from her, in fact. It simply wasn't going to be a part of her home hospice plan.

I think that's such an important note to remember, headed into the next phase of this experience. Each family has to make their own decisions. As a family we had made the decision that worked best for my grandmother and her situation. A different family in a similar situation may have opted to continue using the feeding tube at home, and that would have been okay too. What matters is that you feel contented with your plan and that the patient is as comfortable as they can be. We felt confident in our decision to proceed in the way we felt would keep her most comfortable and less irritated, and for us that meant no more feeding tube.

So, with the plan in place and the papers signed, I drove home to help my uncle get things cleared out and ready for the hospital equipment to arrive. The company delivering it was expected to be there within the hour. It was all happening so fast now. By the time I arrived, he had one of the bedrooms almost entirely cleared out. We then started cleaning, disinfecting, and making this room as cozy as we possibly could. As much as he didn't want to be a part of the bedside vigil, he showed up in such a huge way to prepare this beautiful space for his mom. We laughed and played as we quickly and efficiently prepared her home. With her room done and an abundance of nervous energy to spare, we didn't just stop with that one room. We set up little napping stations throughout the rest of the house for people to sneak away and rest for a few hours. For what it was, we had a pretty comfortable and practical set-up ready to accommodate everyone during that time.

With the equipment on its way and the room ready, we faced our next hurdle. My aunt called from the hospital and said they were faced with a bit of a dilemma. They were having trouble finding an ambulance to transport Gram home. Remember the obituary I had been asked to write a few months back... well that man's son and his wife happen to be first responders who drive the ambulance. One call to them and before the sentence was finished, the wife burst out and said, "We'll head there now. Call and let them know we're on our way." My aunt relayed the message and the hospital employee, in complete disbelief replied, "You must really know the right people. That's beautiful." It was beautiful.

Those same responders were also there the night that Mom had died. They had left their holiday meal to come to our rescue. I had been overjoyed to be able to return the favor by writing his dad's obituary, only to have that kindness come back tenfold when they jumped to our rescue again, instinctively and without a second thought. Some say that a small town is like a big family... I couldn't agree more.

Back at her home, everything was falling into place. The house was ready, the equipment had arrived and was being assembled. Finally, Gram arrived. It felt so much like she was the guest of honor for whatever we had just poured our energy into creating for her. We didn't know what we were doing, only that we cared enough to want to figure it out and make it great for her. We were rolling with the punches and absolutely making it up as we went along. But, to quote LL Cool J in the 90's, "we were doin it and doin it and doin it well."

After we got her settled in, we all took a breath, looked at each other and collectively realized and acknowledged that we were all very unsure about what would happen next. What we did know was that we were there together for whatever that meant. I intended to be there for the duration. I didn't want to miss a single moment of our last days together. I wasn't given that time with my mom, and while we didn't have a lot of unfinished conversations, who doesn't still want the opportunity to soak up all of your final moments with someone you love most in this world! I wasn't missing the opportunity to spend that time with my grandmother, knowing our days were numbered. My husband, his dad, and our beautiful neighbor covered childcare that week so that I could focus on my Gram in those final days. It takes a village, and I was so grateful for ours!

One member of our village from that night, however, we could have done without. We now affectionately refer to her as "The Hospice Nurse from Hell." And before I continue, please know that especially after that week with Gram, I have the complete and utmost respect for the hospice health care system. It truly is a remarkable, beautiful thing to be a part of. Those individuals made all the difference in the world to us, but more importantly to my grandmother that week, and also partially inspired this book. It really is just the most beautiful, helpful, supportive bridge between worlds. Having said that...

This nurse, though... this woman showed up to the house around 10pm. It had taken us until then to get Gram home and settled in and to be at a point where we could meet with the nurse. She was not shy about her irritation at being on call and having to drive about an hour to get to us, late on a Saturday night. She opened her computer and without ever meeting or even looking at my grandmother, she sat with her head down and asked me a series of ridiculous questions that did not need to be answered out loud by us, but that would have been answered with a quick and simple assessment of the patient. For example, she started with, "Hmm... I see in here that there's a script for a new inhaler. Would you say she's having any difficulty breathing?" Looking around the room at all of our family members and back to her still with her head down, I responded "Well... she just came home on hospice to die of lung cancer. I suppose you can say she is having some difficulty breathing, yes."

She went on to ask me on a scale of 1-10 what I estimated my grandmother's depression level to be. Struggling to see the point, I responded, "well, again, she is aware that her life is ending. I would guess her depression level is relatively high right now." She looked up for the first time in a while and said back to me, "Hmm... well a ten is actively crying. Would you say that the patient is actively crying?" I looked at my cousin and Aunt on the couch across from me as if to say nonverbally, "This bitch..." before replying out loud to her, "Well then why don't you put whichever answer you feel is correct since I don't seem to have the answer you're looking for."

About that time my grandmother needed to use the bathroom. Here's the thing to know about that moment... it occurred to me as I walked in to help my aunt, that I had absolutely no idea in the world what I was doing. We had a bed pan. I didn't know how to even begin to use it or to position her, though. All I could suddenly imagine was hurting her frail body or tearing her skin. We fumbled around for quite some time as that nurse sat with her nose in the computer in the living room, fully aware that we were struggling. Finally, I just declared, "You know... I have no idea what I'm doing or how to help, but I'm willing to bet that the hospice nurse fifteen feet away might be able to tell us how to help her. With that, my cousin asked her if she might get up and come offer some guidance. Reluctantly, she walked to the doorway, looked at us and said, "You're really just better off using adult briefs at this point." I can't even describe to you the rage I felt in that moment and the lack of empathy and initiative this nurse showed up with. I said, "Great suggestion, do you think since we have her naked and she needs to go right now that you might assist this one time?!?" Shockingly, she absolutely did not. She sort of shrugged her shoulders, walked away and went to sit back down in the living room. We muddled through it eventually and had a few awkward laughs along the way. We didn't know what we were doing, just that we wanted to help and that we were committed to figuring it out.

I looked at my cousin and said out loud, "I'm tagging you in, I can't do this shit anymore," and he took over answering questions. I walked back the hall to compose myself. A minute later I hear her ask him if the head of the bed was elevated and deciding to just have some fun with it now, he leans back in his chair, looks into the room that she's in, and replies, "Yep, looks like it's at about a 37-degree angle." Unbelievably, she responds with "Hmm… well 45 is really more desirable." He threw his hands in the air and came back that hall laughing to me as fast as he could get there. We just stood in the bathroom with the door closed for a minute hysterically laughing at the seemingly endless Saturday Night Live skit we seemed to have found ourselves in the middle of.

We walked back out and she finally said to me, "Okay, I will put in the order for her meds and they should be here by Tuesday." Tuesday?!? I literally laughed and looked at her as I hit my limit and said, "Tuesday?! Today is Saturday... She may not even be here Tuesday. I'm not sure what's happening right now, but it seems as if you're not even familiar with your job right now. These are medicines she is going to need immediately tonight now that we are home." She disputed with me and told me no doctor was on call and they would have to wait until Monday when normal hours resumed! Dear lord... grant me the strength. I just looked at her and finally said, "Okay, here's the deal... you do have an on-call doctor and here is her name. You call her, she calls the 24-hour pharmacy, and they deliver it directly here tonight. However, we have enough left over from when my grandfather was home and on hospice care to get her through tonight and tomorrow until we can talk with anyone else. You need to leave now." She started to stammer and tell us she wasn't done yet, of course to which I interrupted and repeated, "I'm sorry but you need to go now. We have wasted enough time with this nonsense tonight, almost three hours now. Her time is precious and uncertain. We're done for tonight." as I escorted her out of the house.

She left around midnight that night and we all just stayed in the living room for a few minutes digesting and processing what had just happened and laughing about the complete absurdity of the whole situation. We had decided then that humor was going to be our coping mechanism and bonding agent. For now, the bar had been set at, "She may not even be here on Tuesday."

Fair warning, as the week would go on, the humor would get proportionally darker and darker.

Permission to Laugh at a Funeral

Permission to Laugh at a Funeral

Queen of Sheba

We all made it through that first night and managed to even catch a few hours of sleep in shifts. We had no idea what to expect or for how long to expect it, but we were all committed to doing what was needed. That next morning, Sunday morning, my uncle showed up, ready to prepare a giant breakfast spread for everyone. Having everyone just jump in however and wherever they felt comfortable and useful was proving to be such a remarkable system. The hospice supervisor and LPN arrived for a visit early that morning. First, we made them sit and eat with us before talking business. We did, however, talk about the nurse from the previous night over our bacon. They were both in complete disbelief that the first nurse had behaved in such a manner, and that she didn't have Gram's meds there the night before. One quick phone call and her comfort kit of meds was on the way to her within the hour. That visit with those nurses was happy, joyful, and bright. They were kind and gentle with her, and completely compassionate to the situation and everyone involved. They showed us so much grace and beauty during those moments.

That day brought many visitors and precious time spent with the great grand kids, creating beautiful memories. It also brought with it a toast! You heard me right... all Gram wanted to do was drink a little beer and have a toast to family! So, we put a little beer (and a tiny dash of the thickening to assure she wouldn't aspirate it) in her hospital sippy cup. We all cracked open a beer and joined her in a toast to life and to family. I know that I had decided consciously to soak up all of the moments, good and bad, but at this point it was very hard for everyone involved not to see the beautiful moments happening all around us. It was peaceful and full of love and support - the very ideal definition of family.

The same cousin who had sung *Amazing Grace* so eloquently at my mom's funeral showed up to pray and to sing - this time, for her dying Aunt. That was truly her way of showing love. She went into her room and sang so beautifully for her. We were present, and listening from the next room, but gave them a little space to share that moment just between them. Gram seemed so at peace listening to her sing. While writing this book I talked to my cousin and asked her what she sang that day. She sort of giggled and just told me she let the lord take the reins and sang whichever words just flowed through her... I asked her more specifically though, what did she feel moved to sing in that moment, and she replied, "That's just the thing... I was making it up as I was singing it to her." It turned out to be just as much of a transformative moment for her singing as it was for my grandmother, or any of us who had been listening, for that matter. She did tell me, though, that she remembers singing about the peace and beauty of spiritually and returning home. She wasn't able to remember the words, specifically, just the way it felt.

Later that evening when the grandkids were there, inspired by our cousin singing, they performed their own Christmas caroling in the room with Grandma too. Tiny voices surrounding her bed, a giant smile on her face; this was the good stuff. This woman had come home, as she had requested, and was surrounded by an endless stream of love throughout her final days. What more could you ask for?

Late Sunday night, like middle of the night late, a car pulled into my gram's driveway. We had been expecting my aunt, but instead it was her daughter. My cousin, who happens to be a nurse, walked through the door and said, "Hey guys... I work night shift and I'm off tonight. I can't sleep so I thought I would stop by and see if you need any help or a little nap." I could have kissed her face! She was the breath of fresh air I needed in that moment. I gave her the med schedule and quickly fell asleep for four glorious hours! She took a nap after I got up. That afternoon when we were both awake, she decided that she didn't actually mind hanging out the next couple of days while she was off. This made me so incredibly happy - happy to have that time with her, but also happy because the system we had developed as a family was proving to be pretty fool-proof and very efficient. At some point that day, she and I had a conversation with our Gram - just the two of us with her. As we sat with her, we asked her if there was anything she wanted or needed, and similarly to the toast from the day before, we asked if she wanted to hit the bowl one last time. After careful consideration, she told us "I'd better not. It might actually kill me this time." Hahaha, fair enough. So, we joked with her, but also very seriously told her that we would be in charge of med distribution and that we promised her wholeheartedly she would not be in any discomfort if we could help it. It was an amazing moment of solidarity and security for her, knowing that we had her back and that we were going to help guide her through this gracefully.

That day we playfully nicknamed Gram *The Queen of Sheba* because she just laid there on her "throne" being waited on hand and foot, and being pampered just as much. She got a full body massage to make her skin and muscles feel soft. Her daughter, who was a hair stylist by trade, took her time and lovingly washed her mother's hair, dried and styled it for her – making her look absolutely radiant. Turns out she was much better at parting and styling Gram's hair than I was! We also gave her a little mani / pedi to have her looking her very best for when her *big day* arrived. Something that I have not often shared, is that the last night we had all been on the porch talking and laughing with my mom, she mentioned that she desperately needed a pedicure. As that was just several days before she passed away, she didn't have the chance to get that pedicure. Several times during the days following her death, I contemplated going to the funeral home and painting her toenails for her. Ultimately, and I cannot remember why, I decided not to go. I have always regretted that on some small level. Isn't it always the things we don't end up saying or doing that we regret, though?? So now, with some time to prepare for my grandmother's death, I was elated to dote over her and to paint her nails to make sure she felt her absolute best during that time.

By this point, our family had a groove, and we were functioning like a well-oiled machine! We had shifts; we were utilizing the napping stations; we were being well fed; most importantly, we were filled with love for each other and, of course, for her. Strangely, we were enjoying every second of our extended family sleepover, much more than anyone could have anticipated! Although, there were people in and out to see her fairly constantly those few days, the rest of the time was just family time, spent lounging around together, hanging out with Gram and living what was left of her life with her.

One of her neighbors stopped to see her, and by this point it was becoming more difficult for my grandmother to speak. I couldn't make out what she was trying to tell me, and as her frustration grew, her voice became even more hoarse. She was finally able to get out a frustrated little raspy growl that I was to "get her a beer." She was scolding me for not offering her friend a cold one right as she walked through the front door. Silly me, where were my manners? We all had a good laugh. I did of course, go get everyone a cold one, fixed up another sippy cup (from which she wouldn't take any more than a taste or two) and let her enjoy a beer with her friend just as she would have on any other day!

Also that day we called Gram's ex-husband, my biological grandfather, to ask if he wanted the opportunity to come and say goodbye to her and to just be with his kids, as they faced this all head on. After all, they created three human beings together and shared a lot of life for a while. Regardless of divorce and many years apart, we thought the opportunity for him to be a small part of that family moment only seemed appropriate. He did want to see her. When he arrived, we gave them their privacy to say goodbye. Or at least I swear to you that was our intention. It was short lived, however, when we all sat down in the living room and soon discovered that the baby monitor we had placed near her pillow, and kept in the living room so we could always hear her without always hovering, was still on and picking up their voices quite clearly, or at least his anyway. My Uncle's wife reached for it to turn it off – and I'm not sure whether to tell you I'm ashamed or proud of my actions – but I told her with deep conviction that she should set that monitor right back down and let their kids hear this final moment between their parents. I knew if I had that opportunity with my parents, I would have taken it.

She set the receiver back down and as a family we listened to some of their final words to each other... We didn't listen to all of it, but we heard enough to know that at some point, there had been real love between them. What we did listen to was a peaceful, healing goodbye that happened in that room that day.

Tuesday... Tuesday of that week was a great day!

Permission to Laugh at a Funeral

Hidden Strength

As we approached Wednesday, Gram was beginning to fade out a little more. She wanted to rest more, but didn't always want to completely surrender to sleep. She had a few more visitors during the day – some childhood friends, former coworkers, neighbors, family...it was really something to see people want to honor her and to see her one last time. I can tell you, if you're in that situation and you hesitate to go because it might be awkward or you might not know what to say, just go. Figure it out when you get there. Make it up as you go along. But go. Just show up and let them know they touched your life and will not be forgotten.

While she was enjoying the company that day, by evening time she knew she was starting to get much worse. She asked me to get her husband and bring him to her. She suddenly became incredibly insistent that I bring him to see her. I hated that moment of having to tell her bad news, but I gently looked at her and as softly as I could, I stroked her hair and told her that it just wasn't possible to have him make that trip. He was about 45 minutes away, and physically he could not handle the travel, the excitement, and the exertion of it all. A panic attack with the inability to breathe for him was a definite certainty.

Still, she pleaded with me. She gripped me tightly and told me she needed to see him. I empathized with her, but she became more upset and told me that all of this was just so cruel. It did seem cruel that she couldn't see her husband one last time. Talk about pressure. I hated seeing her so sad, and feeling powerless. I walked outside onto the porch, and we gathered for a family meeting. We weighed the risks of having him travel to her, knowing that it very well could result in his death as well. We decided it was worth the risk. If he died after making the trip to see her, as she was dying too... would that be the most awful ending in the world? Nicholas Sparks, and millions of Nicholas Sparks fans, myself included, would argue it is not.

We quickly devised a plan. I was unwilling to leave her side, but my sister and our cousin were both nurses. Another cousin was willing to drive. They decided one nurse would ride along to pick him up, and the other would ride back with them hopefully to return him home safely after their visit. That way there were two people with him at all times, one of whom is a nurse. With the plan in place, I called the nursing home to let him know that it was time and that she would like to see him. As expected, he became very upset, and almost immediately his breathing started to become erratic. I calmed him down as much as I could over the phone. He said that he wanted to see her and that he would have the nurse help him get ready while my cousins were on their way to get him.

No sooner were they ready to leave, though and his nurse called. He was in a full-blown panic attack and was struggling to breathe. We all had to conclude and accept that it would not be practical for him to travel. He was distraught. My gram was distraught. I wanted to be with him and stay with her. It was a miserable, helpless feeling until... Until I asked the nurse if she could stay with him and help him calm down enough that we could facilitate a phone conversation between them. Given the circumstances it would not be easy, but it would prove to be the most worthwhile thing I had done, maybe to date.

I walked back into Gram's room, sat down beside her side, and explained that he physically could not make the trip to come, despite our absolute best efforts. I explained that the nurse was getting him prepared to talk to her, though, and that I would help them have one last conversation on the phone with each other. At this point, she was very hard to understand, and it required focus and attentiveness on my part to figure out what she was saying. It had become difficult to understand my grandfather, as well. I seemed to speak his language fluently, though.

As soon as he was calm and ready to talk, the nurse called me back. In the meantime, my cousins and my sister and I had been on the porch just swept up in the gravity of what was happening and trying to stay composed. Once the nurse put him on the phone, he and I talked privately for a minute and then I walked back inside to let them talk to each other. Walking into that room, for that purpose, was the heaviest thing I have ever done. Heavier even than telling her the end was nearing, because now it was actually here.

I had put him on speaker phone as we all walked in to Gram's room together. Already in there were our parents and my father-in-law, whose face I remember distinctly. I'm not sure who else might have been there because to successfully do what I did next, I had to disconnect from the entire experience, and just maintain a level of duty and service. I couldn't invest myself personally in order for it to work. I held the phone near Gram's face and listened closely as she and her husband went back and forth professing their undying love for each other and recalling the things they most cherished about each other. If I'm being truthful, I can't tell you most of what they said in those moments. At one point during their conversation, I made the mistake of looking up and my gaze landed on my father-in-law, a man in his sixties who could barely breathe because he was so moved by what was happening. As tears rolled heavily down his face, I quickly realized that every person in that room was being deeply affected. I had to just stare down at the blanket and focus on decoding and dictating, to each of them, what their partner wanted them to hear most in those final moments.

I wouldn't have traded the opportunity to give them that final conversation for anything in this world; but man was that heavy! When they were finished, I felt the need to immediately exit the room, walk outside, and take a few deep breaths to help cleanse the palette from that one, so we could all keep on keeping on.

I thought for sure that that would have been the most heart-wrenching part of that day, but I was wrong. The most authentically raw moment of that entire experience came later that evening. She knew that she was ready to go, and we knew that she was about to leave us. She was tired and her time was coming to an end.

After things had quieted down, I walked into her room and sat down beside her. I knew that I was about to engage in my last waking conversation with my grandmother. I asked her if she had any last-minute logistics to be handled, or any remaining wishes that we could grant for her. There wasn't really anything left for her to do. She seemed very peaceful and content.

As we sat there quietly together, I just looked at her with such love, and I thanked her for everything that she had ever done for me and for always being so genuine and real with me. I'll admit, when I opened my mouth to speak, those words felt awkward and silly at first. I closed my eyes and exhaled. I reminded myself that if I couldn't be authentic and real in the moments where honesty counts most, then what am I even doing? Why on Earth should it feel awkward or uncomfortable telling someone how you feel about them... ever really, but especially in their final moments?? I took another deep breath and just continued talking to her, soul to soul. I told her that she was the strongest person I have ever known and that she was handling this all with such grace. She put her hand on my hand and grabbed it as tightly as she could. With a smile and a slow, raspy whisper she managed to get out, "You... are tougher than I am." Then she exhaled, closed her eyes and smiled. Aside from one final I love you to each other, those were her final words to me. Later that night she faded out and was no longer mentally present with us.

Permission to Laugh at a Funeral

Permission to Laugh at a Funeral

The Nitty Gritty

The next few days brought with them a lot less fun than the previous days, a lot more dark humor, and a lot more love and respect for each other - more than we could have ever imagined. Circling back to everyone having their role in the home hospice experience, and it working out so brilliantly... My cousin who had arrived late Sunday night to help, ended up not leaving the entire week. She made the most excellent tag team partner you can imagine. When it came time to do things like clean her dentures, keep her mouth moist, or even insert suppositories to help with her fever, she jumped right in without any hesitation at all.

In keeping our promise to our grandmother from a few days prior, we kept a very close watch over her. Especially now that she could no longer communicate with us. If her body even flinched or she showed any slight sign of pain or discomfort whatsoever, she was given a little morphine to help ease her body again. We also went through a regular and thorough checklist to see if we could do anything externally to help ease her discomfort as well.

Very early Friday morning, I was sitting bedside just being present and acknowledging that this was all about to come to an end. The same cousin, who had helped answer questions with the hospice nurse that first night, walked into the house. He looked at me and simply said, "I'm just popping my head in quick on my way to work, but I wanted to let you know in person that you demolished the line for dark humor with your picture last night! Congratulations." I had absolutely no idea what he was talking about. He said something like, "I'm off now, but check your phone."

As soon as he was out the door, I immediately checked my phone. Here's the deal... the evening before, my nurse cousin had left for a few hours to check in with her kids. While she was at her home, she sent me a message checking in on things. When I got her message, I had just walked in from outside and sat down next to my grandmother, to have some quiet time with her and to write her obituary. In hindsight, exhaustion and slight delirium were setting in by this point in the week. In response to my cousin's message, I simply took a selfie - smiling and flashing a peace sign, or a thumbs up, or something jovial to let her know nothing had changed and that everything was still fine. As I was taking the photo, my uncle happened to walk in the room, sort of shook his head, but just said, "Hey... you do you." I sort of laughed at that time but really didn't think twice about it all beyond that moment... until my cousin said he was off to work but to check my phone.

To try and understand what he meant, I reread my messages from the night before, which included that photo I had sent. Immediately when I looked at the photo, I became completely and utterly mortified!! What had earned me 'darkest humor moment' of the week?! My carefree selfie that I sent to assure her that things were good, also happened to include my grandmother in all of her end-of-life glory in the background - mouth wide open, eyes closed, hospital bed... the whole nine yards. I had inadvertently posed with her very corpse-like body in the background while I flashed a simple peace sign as if I was on the beach in July! What else do you say except, "Holy shit," and "That was not on purpose!" Too late, what was done was done, though. That night my cousins, rightfully so, earned the right to never let me hear the end of that one!

A few hours later, after the shock and laughter from the photo wore off, and complete physical and emotional exhaustion were setting in, my cousin and tag team partner in all of this, sat at our grandmother's bedside with me, just the three of us again. We had a candid conversation about how long this process might last – as this timeline was completely unpredictable and had already exceeded what any of us had anticipated. I very seriously asked my cousin if the oxygen our grandmother was on, which we realized then was still set fairly high, could be keeping her body from fully letting go.

By this time, we had now spent days watching and monitoring her very closely and we were acutely aware that there were no longer any signs of responsiveness and that there hadn't been for quite some time. We placed the pulse / ox monitor on her finger to test our theory. We gently slipped the oxygen down, away from her nose, to be able to evaluate how well she was breathing on her own. We quickly watched her authentic oxygen level plummet.

Her oxygen had dropped to almost 40 when my Dad walked in the room. He saw that we had moved her oxygen and he panicked a little, or a lot really. He responded as if we were suffocating her with a pillow, which I'm sure to him seemed like we were. He didn't want her to suffer or to feel one ounce of pain. We certainly didn't want that either. If, however, she was ready to transition on and that machine pumping oxygen into her body was keeping her from being able to do that, then we wanted to set her free from it.

We gently placed her oxygen tube back into position and we walked out into the living room, to hold a family meeting, just the two of us with our respective parents. We sat them down and told them that we had tested our theory and that we strongly believed that the oxygen was playing at least some role in keeping her alive. We asked them, on behalf of her, to make peace with letting her go and proceeding with that today. What a humbling parent / child moment, as we found ourselves navigating our parents through that impossible situation. They weren't objecting to the suggestion, but they were naturally hesitant. That decision came with a heavy weight of responsibility. They decided they were ready and able to let go, but that ultimately, they would feel more comfortable hearing from a hospice nurse or doctor that it would not cause her any agony.

We waited patiently and quietly with our parents that day. The hospice nurse came that afternoon and told us that turning the oxygen off would be fine, as it was considered a comfort measure. The doctor on the phone didn't believe it would make much difference one way or another. With that all having been said, our parents decided that at 5pm that evening we would turn off the oxygen and let her body surrender to the end. Most of our family was present that evening, spread throughout the house. My dad and my aunt took turns sharing time together bedside with their mom. Despite its hilarious and humiliating start, Friday had turned into a somber, but beautiful and deliberate day.

During a tender moment with my dad as he sat bedside and just watched his mother sleep... I found myself overcome with the desire to say a few things to him. I sat behind him and gently put my hand on his back. I found it easy and effortless in that moment to tell him that when she dies, he may be fearful and want to react at first. I softly reminded him that the moment she takes her last breath is actually the moment that we were waiting for, and that she was ready for whatever comes next and was looking forward to it even. I'm not sure why I felt compelled to say those things to him, but when she took a big gasp of air he quickly turned to me, slightly panicked, and yelled for his sister. I smiled reassuringly and put my hand on his shoulder. He immediately relaxed back down into his chair as she gasped again. We knew it wasn't quite the end, not just yet. His sister came running and asked if it was time. I softly replied that the breath before wasn't quite it, but that it was coming very soon.

The family gathered around her as we all just sat in silence and watched her. Moments later she did in fact take her final breath here on this Earth. The emotion felt in that room that night was palpable. It was somber for sure, but it wasn't terribly sad. In all honesty, all I could imagine that night was that beautiful group of people she had envisioned, of which so many of our loved ones were included, waiting to embrace her on the next phase of her soul's journey – whatever that may be. It did genuinely feel like a birth, in reverse. Perhaps when a soul is born into a human body there are people who are saddened to see it leave too, but then it's greeted by a room full of people overjoyed to see it arrive here. In this case, her soul was leaving her human body, and we were saddened to see it leave; however, she was now greeted by a huge group of smiling faces, overjoyed to see her arrive.

After sitting together in a collective moment of silence, we slowly filtered out of her room, exhaled and started handling the logistical nitty gritty that came next: the funeral planning, the cremation, comforting and spending time with my grandfather. There might have been a slight break in the clouds, but the storm wasn't quite over yet.

Permission to Laugh at a Funeral

Miss Me, But Let Me Go

Gram didn't want an elaborate service after she died. She wanted close friends and family to gather and celebrate life together, in her honor. We held a brief and small service for her at the funeral home and then a Penn State Tailgate themed Celebration of Life Dinner, because she was an avid college football fan! The celebration wouldn't have been complete without enjoying a little karaoke after dinner! She was always known for getting up and singing or making music. It only made sense to send her off with everyone's favorite open mic jam!

One of our distant relatives traveled into town for the service, and as she arrived to the funeral home, she asked how she could help. I told her that she could carry the memorial photo boards in from my car and set them up. She went to grab them, and I went on to doing something else, never giving them a second thought. I could see later that they were displayed, so what more did I need to know about it? Halfway through the service though, the same cousin who reminded me at my mom's viewing that someone had asked me if she just killed over, now approached me laughing hysterically. We had repurposed the photo boards from my mom's service and had a couple of boards leftover with Mom's photos still on them that we didn't end up using. I never thought to tell her not to grab all of the boards, and so, scattered around the funeral home were some displays of my grandma and her life, and a couple of just my mom's life – with some extended family photos sprinkled in. Not many people even noticed that some of the boards didn't belong, but we laughed like crazy! We decided it should be a silly tradition, to carry over and randomly place one funeral board from each deceased family member to display with the next to pass away.

My grandmother was not religious, nor did she want a formal funeral. We honored her wishes and kept it short and sweet. At the end of the open viewing, everyone who was still present gathered in a huddle in front of her casket. We intended to read a quick poem and say a prayer. I remember trying to read aloud and the sheer reality and emotion of the situation overcame me as we all stood together in that group. I'm not sure if it was a relative or our friend from the funeral home who stepped in to read for me, but somebody gracefully jumped in and took over as I surrendered to and fully embraced the words and the collective emotions of that moment. If there was one gift that Gram had given us at the end of her life it was unity… and it was beautiful.

After the service we gathered for a meal, sang some karaoke and just enjoyed a little time together. Her wishes were to be cremated and to have her ashes scattered at many of the same locations as her husband, so we made the decision to just wait and spread her ashes after he had also passed. As we closed the chapter on the 2nd Annual Mills Family Christmas Funeral, we found ourselves approaching our first holiday without our mom and now our grandmother. Gram had died on December 7th. We now found ourselves diving headfirst into a month of creating magic for our kids, despite the mountain of grief and loss we were facing behind the scenes.

Miss Me, But Let Me Go
Christina Rossetti

When I come to the end of the road
And the sun has set for me
I want no rites in a gloom filled room
Why cry for a soul set free?

Miss me a little, but not for long
And not with your head bowed low
Remember the love that once we shared
Miss me, but let me go.

For this is a journey we all must take
And each must go alone.
It's all part of the master plan
A step on the road to home.

When you are lonely and sick at heart
Go to the friends we know.
Laugh at all the things we used to do
Miss me, but let me go.

Permission to Laugh at a Funeral

All I Want For Christmas Is You

With so much sadness and uncertainty in the air it was hard to know and decide what to do that holiday season. Do we carry on as if nothing happened? Do we go even bigger because they aren't here? We certainly weren't going to *not* celebrate... it had been our mom's favorite holiday after all. When she was a young girl her house had burned down just a couple of weeks before Christmas and her family lost everything. They all temporarily moved in with her uncle. That year, she told me, was the very reason she came to love Christmas so much. They had just lost everything and she was feeling sad and afraid. That was, until her entire community came together and showered her family with love, support and extra special gifts for that holiday season. As an adult, she told me that she remembered feeling the most holiday spirit that she had ever felt during that trying time in her life. As a result, she was always the first to want to recreate that for others any time she was able to. It's safe to say that Mom's legacy - along with our sweet, precious girls - kept everyone going that holiday season. The show must go on, after all, and those girls were busy being beautiful little humans, filled with love and wonder.

My daughter performed in *The Nutcracker* that year for the first time. Despite being one of my proudest Mommy moments, watching her in that show was extremely difficult for me. My Mom loved to watch her dance and when we all sat together at the show a year prior, Mom couldn't stop talking about being excited to watch her on stage in that show someday. Now a year later, watching her on stage, without my mom cheering from the audience, was quite the mix of happy and sad emotions. One of my mom's closest friends had a granddaughter who was also in the show. At the end of opening night, she approached me to say hello and dote over the girls. I couldn't even look at her without bursting into tears. Every time I looked at her, I saw how much she missed my Mom and what amazing friends they were. All these years later, in fact, I can still barely hug her at performances without needing a quiet moment to put myself back together after. I think some people are just a tangible reminder of what has been lost, and the love that those people have left behind. For me, her friend is one of those tangible, ever-present reminders. I feel that love when she looks at me and it is still the most bittersweet pain every time.

As it turned out, we ended up with two trees in our house that Christmas. We kept our tradition of cutting down a tree from the local tree farm to set up and decorate in the living room. Also, though, the girls and I went to my parent's attic and dug out an old artificial tree and all of my mom's Disney holiday decorations from when we were young. We laughed so much that day as we set up her whole display in a different room of our house for everyone to enjoy. This collection had always been one of my parents' proudest and most elaborate holiday décor setups. It was bright, cheerful, and made everyone smile when they saw it assembled again and on display.

Having lost his wife and his mother, my dad had no interest in the holiday at all, much less decorating. My sister was instrumental in keeping so many sentimental touches alive, in general, but especially that first holiday season. She was persistent with our dad, reminding him of the importance of the holiday to our family, and expressing the need for our girls to carry on, business as usual. It was Mom's favorite holiday after all.

One day our dad went on one of his retail therapy shopping trips. When he came home, he had a new outlook and a ridiculous amount of holiday items to decorate the new tree which he had also just bought. He could not have been prouder of that shopping trip! He had put so much love and thought into designing the tree that year. He bought a black artificial tree and these gorgeous ivory ornaments for on it. Many of the ornaments were tiny picture frames that he filled with photos of her. He had found a way to reclaim control and celebrate the holidays in a way that felt best to him.

He honored her that year by creating a Memorial Christmas tree, and it was absolutely breathtaking! Not only did we get to see a glimpse of his authentic, creative side again, we also made the new memories of decorating with him and our girls and making an evening out of it! It was perfect. Our parents were always known for their themed Christmas trees each year. That year, the theme was Bonita. We couldn't have felt her presence and her beautiful legacy surrounding us any more than we did that season.

My Aunt Shell (my dad's sister), also went out of her way to surround us with so much love during this time too. She had just lost her mom, as well, and we were all looking for a way to create new holiday magic. She opened up her home and hosted our first annual holiday cookie baking day! Wow was that the thing we all needed and hadn't known it!! We laughed, cried, drank mimosas and margaritas, danced – because it's scientifically proven that dancing while you bake makes better cookies – and really just had the absolute best time all together! We let the kids have full creative freedom with the sugar cookie dough and what we ended up with was an epic "create your own turd cookie" contest! These sweet, angelic little girls could not stop laughing as they added cocoa powder, sprinkles, etc to make the most realistic looking poop cookie they each could! Non- stop laughter filled the kitchen. We were grateful to be alive and to have each other in that moment. It felt good to be reminded that life can be really difficult at times, but it's still really, really good too!

In general, I was really struggling during this time if I'm being honest. I was operating on autopilot. I was doing what was necessary, but not much beyond that. I was spending time regularly at the nursing home and maintained constant communication with them about the most important things that happened throughout my grandfather's days. I was learning to find room to breathe and to create a new routine in the middle of such present sadness. I remember stopping at the movie theater near the nursing home one night after I had left there. I just needed to sit and not think about my own reality for a few hours. It was my first time in a theater in a little while, and my first time in there alone in a very long time. It's a strange thing to embrace social settings by yourself if you're not accustomed to it. I felt a little awkward until I sat down in an almost empty theater and simply thought to myself, "This experience was created for my entertainment right now. I'm just going to unplug and enjoy it." And I really did! It felt so freeing and so satisfying to just sit down, eat snacks and get lost in someone else's story!

At some point that December, I had a few things I needed to take care of. I had to deal with some lingering issues from my mom's cell phone and I also wanted to make *a Build A Bear* for my sister with a recording of my mom's voice inside. As much as I wanted to do those things, they were heavy tasks! Beautiful, sweet, Daniel, who had helped me catch my breath a couple of months prior, jumped in again and made those experiences so much different for me than I was anticipating them to be. As he listened to me tell him about what I needed and wanted to do, he quickly suggested that we go together and make a fun day of it.

I was torn at first, feeling like I might need to be alone to really feel and fully process it all. I quickly realized and remembered, though, that his purpose in my life during that time was to help me with the heavy stuff and to make it seem a little lighter. Hopefully, we did that for each other. I know for me, that day, that trip... he certainly made it an entirely different and unexpected experience! I had a few quick somber moments, but they were few and far between... compared to the laughter, joy and just present playfulness that we created together that day. He was silly and completely jovial in moments of pause when dealing with the cell phone agent. He even got lost in the magic of *Build a Bear* with me and ended up making one for his son for Christmas! I knew that my mom had guided him straight into my path, and on that day I was never more sure of it, or more thankful for his friendship and continued presence in my life!

With all of the special gifts bought, the new themed tree decorated, and the final curtain closed on an amazing *Nutcracker* performance, it was time to face the first anniversary of mom's death and all of our first Christmas without our moms.

Christmas day ended up being a smashing success! We gave each other such thoughtful, beautiful gifts and the girls were unaffected. They just carried on as their bright, adorable, happy little selves! The greatest part of that morning, though, was when my sister and I held up identical sized boxes, thinking that it was our annual AAA membership, something Mom always neurotically made sure to get us each year for Christmas! We were absolutely certain as we laughed and tore open the boxes only to find that we had been duped. They were different gifts completely, neither of them being the membership. We moved on from that idea and eventually did open our membership cards. That year, however, they were wrapped in different sized packages and camouflaged so that we could never have been able to guess the contents. It has become such a core memory for me because our dad was so proud of himself in that moment. We looked at him in shock and said, "Hmm… all these years, it's just been wrapped in that big silver box." He smirked at us with all the pride in the world and responded, "Yeah well, I wrapped the gifts this year," and sat back victoriously in his chair, having just absolutely crushed this first impossible holiday without her. He kept her tradition alive that year, yet he did it in a way that was unique to him and that set a new tone entirely.

My sister and I also started our own new tradition that year of making the lasagna together on Christmas Eve so we could just pop it in the oven Christmas Day while we open gifts. It was such a peaceful, healing, productive use of our energy that connected us to our mom and brought us closer together than we had ever been!

My very favorite part of that holiday season was the way we chose to honor our mom and acknowledge that it had been one year since she left us. We live in the middle of town, but we have cousins who live about ten minutes out in the country. They offered to host a paper lantern release in her memory that year. She died at approximately 5:50 in the evening, so we timed the lantern release to be at that specific time one year later. Some of our closest family and friends joined us that evening and all gathered in small groups with lanterns ready to light.

Mariah Carey singing *"O Holy Night"* filled the quiet night air with the perfect melody to release the lanterns... and a year of pain and anguish along with them. I can only speak for myself, but I feel very sure that there was a collective weight lifted off of us as the lanterns rose higher in the night sky and the song became more dramatic... bringing us first metaphorically to our knees and then helping us to rise back up together, surrounded by love and ready to face the promise of a new day.

We had survived the first year without her. Her death had left a giant gaping hole in our lives, but we were rising up despite it and had spent the last year creating so much extra light and love to fill that hole! That Christmas evening as we all quietly watched the lanterns rise, I couldn't have felt more connected to her, to the universe, to each other. Just like those lanterns in that dark night sky, there are just simply some beauties in this world that can only be found in the darkest of times.

With the holidays behind us, the first anniversary of her death out of the way, it was time to try and look for some normalcy again...

Permission to Laugh at a Funeral

Auld Lang Syne

And so, as we turned the page of that year, we began a somber new chapter of irony. My grandfather had once been told that he had an estimated 6 months to live. At this point in the story, 14 months had elapsed. In the meantime, my mom had suddenly left us, and his wife - my adorable grandmother, had faded away as well. Life is weird, you guys. It is weird; and it is beautiful; and it is fragile; and it is unpredictable.

I had never been more aware of that concept than during those months. There were endless curve balls being thrown and I had no choice but to surrender to the process and to try and find the good to hang on tight to. I found myself going back to my mother's mantra in life.

God,

Grant me the serenity to

Accept the things I cannot change

The courage to change the things I can

And the wisdom to know the difference!

Amen

My whole world had been filled with events that I could not control at that time, but here's what I did know. I knew that surrendering the need to control it gave me an insane sense of peace that I had never experienced before. It also gave me mental clarity, or that wisdom that Mom would talk about – the ability to clearly see which things in my world I could navigate and have some control over. I'm also incredibly fortunate to have been raised with the courage and tenacity to never hesitate to act on something that needs addressed, if it's within my power to do so.

First, I started giving myself permission to prioritize myself and to make space to just breathe. Part of that for me was pairing my visits to the nursing home with something purposeful, as often as I could. After my visits with my grandfather, I would go and see a movie, or sit by the water, or on top of the mountain... I could feel myself, day by day, shedding the skin of who I was and preparing to step into a new phase of my life.

Feeling more like my authentic self, more calm and collected, and more aware of what was mine to handle... I was ready to circle back to our divorce. My husband and I had many conversations during the year that we had separated but were still living together. We had listened to each other, even when we didn't agree with what the other was saying. We talked about our fears moving forward and allowed each other to be honest about them. We laughed. We cried. We were hurt, but we were going to be okay and ultimately, we knew we were making the right decision.

We had decided that things had calmed down enough that we could begin moving forward with a divorce. We were no strangers to how strongly and negatively a family can be affected when there isn't a strong base of respect and communication with each other. Neither of us had any desire to create that atmosphere for our families. We adopted the family mantra that "Marriages may end, but families do not." I'm proud to say that we have continued to live by that completely. Sometimes it's just not gonna work, and IF you find yourself at that point, why not find the good and make the most of it to create a situation that's better for both of you, for all of you?! If change has to happen, that much you may not be able to control... but you can control what that change looks like and work together to create a new situation that works better, while also creating the desired necessary changes.

Personally, I did not make the difficult decision to get a divorce only to continue to argue and to be angry. I was solely motivated by peaceful living at that time, and from that day forward! We had one conversation where my husband was expressing his fear of not knowing what to do next. He felt taken advantage of because, in his words, "We bought your grandparent's house, across the street from your parents and beside your sister. You're set up, now what am I supposed to do?" I remember just taking a breath and smiling at him. He wasn't trying to fight with me, he was genuinely asking and trying to figure it out. I just told him not to get ahead of himself. Yes, it was my grandparents' house. Yes, it was next to my family. But, he was still family and those girls would still be growing up in that house. I told him, "You love to landscape and there's so much here to do. You have two kids living with you, I only have one; and honestly – I didn't make the rules, but biologically I am her mom, and anywhere we are together is likely to feel like home with me. I want you to keep the house. I would never want you to feel awkward when you're here that you're outnumbered entering the family neighborhood. I want this to genuinely feel like home for them and for you."

All of those things are true, and that has proven to be the best decision over the past few years, no doubt. But... I was also motivated to have him keep the house because I was feeling desperate for a fresh start, a new beginning. I was more than okay finding a new place to call home, knowing that my daughter is loved and cared for and literally surrounded by love on all sides of her when she spends time at that house with her daddy.

Permission to Laugh at a Funeral

Permission to Laugh at a Funeral

Last Dance with Mary Jane

In late February, as my grandfather's health dramatically declined, my frustration with his health care grew. He was a Vietnam vet who had traveled the world and had himself a good time. That and the fact that he had been on steady morphine for almost two years at this point, made him intolerant to a lot of the medications intended to calm him down and to help him relax. I struggled hard to get an approved increase, especially toward his final days. February 25th of that year I received a crisis phone call from the nursing home telling me that he had been found on the floor of his bedroom again, uninjured but struggling to breathe. This time they were taking him to the local emergency room. I couldn't understand why, as he had a DNR, was a hospice patient, and any comfort measures needed certainly could have been handled by the medical staff on site. It was also his strong wish to not ever be placed on a ventilator, as he was terminal and could not see the point in prolonging the inevitable. These were his wishes. This was the end of his life. These were the moments they had given me the honor of helping guide them through and advocating for them during.

I happened to be in the middle of a massage that afternoon when I got the call. I apologized, abruptly ended the massage, and rushed out immediately to drive straight to the hospital. He was now beginning to actively die. I was confused, as I stood bedside with him, waiting for test results to come back. At one point in his hysteria, before the meds kicked in, he called out in desperation for his mother... and of course, I embraced him and held on tight as he sobbed and looked ahead with fear in his eyes. I held him until he calmed down and eventually fell back to sleep, however, this sleep was restless and filled with agitation. He had been placed on a bi-pap machine upon arrival, and he did not want it on. He was constantly trying to tug at it and remove it.

The doctor came in to present me with the options, as if I were hearing that he was sick for the first time. He was compassionate but confused, almost as if I had been the one who had insisted he be brought there. I explained that I was just as confused as he was about the transfer given that he was a long-term hospice patient in his final days. He finished doing his job, however and explained that we could do one of the following: put him on a ventilator, which he was adamantly against; keep him on bi-pap for a little while, hoping that it might help a little – as he was actively tugging at it as we spoke; or transfer him back to the home to be sedated and kept comfortable until he passed.

Obviously, I decided that we would take him back and resume what I thought we had been doing in the first place. I also decided I was going to go back with him and stay there until we had a consistent and firm medication plan in place. We had been struggling with that issue for long enough and today brought with it a lot of unnecessary chaos for everyone, especially when it could have been avoided if he had been properly medicated. He was dying of lung cancer and COPD. At this point, it had progressed so much that when he was awake and conscious, he felt as if he was suffocating, breathing through a tiny little straw – as it was once explained to me. His oxygen tube, which was crucial to sustaining his life, also filled his body with more CO_2 which he was already having trouble getting rid of. He would wake up, rip off the tube and gasp for air. This would often set in motion a series of ridiculous events, requiring all hands on deck at some points.

Having committed to sitting at his bedside until the issue was resolved, I just wanted him to be able to rest peacefully. He was on hospice, in his final moments. I struggled to understand why we weren't doing a better job at giving him some dignity and ending his panic and fear that he was experiencing when his meds would wear off. I'll tell you though, those moments spent with him in panic and fear when he was reaching the end, as well as the many amazing times with him when we first found out he was dying, were so humbling and really brought life full circle for me. I was his caregiver, and he was a vulnerable, scared person who needed someone to tell him what to do. What a beautiful privilege. In that moment, I had his back. He was finally going to be able to just rest and transition to whatever comes after this life.

That night though... that night would become the most gut-wrenching, yet also the most hilarious of them all. Around 8:30pm I had somewhat of an argument with the nurse on duty when my grandfather was due for his meds. Obviously my goal was to keep him resting peacefully, given the circumstances, and the alternative. The nurse told me that he was PRN (as needed / when asked for) with his meds and that he hadn't asked for them and didn't seem to need them. I took a strong stance and explained to her that, especially in light of that day's events, everyone was very clear that he was experiencing his final days. He was to be kept comfortable and sedated until he passed. He was clearly no longer in a position to ask for them. I affirmed that I was there that night to do that for him until I was sure everyone was on board with the new plan. I also had to advocate for diapers as we made the transition, rather than keeping a catheter in which, by that point, was causing further irritation and agitation.

By the time the nurse finally gave him his next dose he was waking up, just as hostile as anticipated. He ripped the catheter out, took off his oxygen and tried to get out of bed. He wouldn't let anyone near him. I chose to hang back and let him have some space, as he was understandably completely irrational in those moments. A male nurse kept trying to reason with him and put his oxygen back on him. I repeatedly told the nurse that it was okay for him to not wear it. I explained that oxygen was deemed a comfort measure and that if he didn't want it, nobody was doing anything wrong by letting him take it off. That nurse went to him one more time to put the oxygen back on him, disregarding what I had just said. My grandfather punched straight ahead, full steam, straight at this man's testicles. That nurse gasped for air and then looked straight over at me. I just reminded him that it was okay for my grandfather to sit in that chair without his oxygen on. Even if he were to refuse the oxygen, continue to sit in that chair and take his last breath, that is a reality that we were prepared for.

That might sound callus or uncaring, but really it was quite the opposite. It was coming from a place of love, understanding and acceptance that this process was happening, and that this was not the best way for it to be handled. Nobody was listening, though. His breathing became shallow and more erratic, as he began to panic more. He took off full speed out of his room and down the hall. There was nothing graceful about this and he wouldn't let anyone near him. Everyone was kind of scrambling at this point, and I had become fully irritated that it had gotten to this level again.

I walked behind him and stopped in front of him when he finally leaned against the wall to rest. Usually, I was very effective at calming him. That night though... well, that night instead of breathing with me, he took another quick full force jab, this time straight at the front of my throat.

I matched him right back with a slightly different side of that same loving maternal energy I had given him in the hospital earlier that afternoon. This time, however, it looked like me guiding his shoulders as he was collapsing and sliding down the wall. I told him he could sit right there until he calmed down and was ready for help, but that he could not continue hitting people. I had the staff get his oxygen and a wheelchair for when he was calm and ready. A few minutes later he was calming down, and I got him back up into the chair, then I made the need for stronger medication abundantly clear.

We sat in the quiet, dimly lit common area of that home for quite a while that night. He wasn't able to really say very much but we didn't need to. Sometimes just sharing space with someone and feeling their energy is enough.

He had spent most of his life as a landscaper, and as we sat in that space together looking out at the night sky, he noticed and then needed to touch and to feel the dirt in the plants near the window. I was amazed at how those were still his instincts, despite being in such a confused, altered state of mind. I wasn't nearly as amazed though, as I was at what happened next.

He was in his wheelchair now, blanket around his shoulders, oxygen back on, holding a cup of ice chips they had just given him. I was in the chair next to him, quietly observing him, taking in the realness and the gravity of all of it. There had been a lot of heavy days recently, but this one was pretty damn heavy, ending with a literal throat punch that I could still feel.

All of a sudden, as if on a mission, he put the cup of ice between his knees and took a piece of ice from the cup with his right hand. Using his left hand, he made a fist with his thumb side up, and he jammed the ice chip down into his fist. (Picture a magician stuffing the handkerchief into their hand.) I was fascinated, wondering what he was doing and I couldn't stop watching him. Once the ice chip was jammed down into his left fist, he moved his left hand closer to his face and used his right hand as if he was holding a lighter and was trying to light the bowl he just packed full {of ice chips.} Once I realized what he was doing, I burst out laughing. Hearing my laughter, he paused and looked up at me which took him out of his altered state and brought him back to the reality of that moment. With direct eye contact, he simply shrugged his shoulders as he started belly laughing too. We took a few deep breaths together and then he was calm, comfortable, ready to lay back down and get some sleep.

What an amazing gift he gave me that night, to see him revert back to his truest self for a moment – not only digging around in the plants, but also instinctively trying to smoke a bowl again, even if it was just one full of ice chips. To him, those ice chips were his last dance with Mary Jane, and that was good enough for a shared little giggle and a smile.

The next day his doctor apologized for what had happened the day and night before. He assured me in that moment that hospice protocols were now fully in place. They had also implemented "No Veteran Dies Alone" which meant that he was nearing the end of his life, and when someone from his family wasn't able to be there, an RN would be at his side (around the clock) until he passed. Also, a new nurse came on that day and quietly pulled me aside. She told me that she completely understood my frustration and the need to manage his meds better. She assured me that during her time there, she would make sure that he received his meds a little ahead of schedule to ensure that there would be no more incidents like the day before.

I stayed again that night because I needed to confirm it for myself, and let's be honest... I also really wanted to spend this time with him. It tore my heart out, no lie, but I felt like I was continuing to help my grandmother take care of him and continuing to honor the responsibilities they had both entrusted me with. He was now finally sedated and resting peacefully.

A few days later, I went back to check in and spend a little time with him. While cleaning my grandparents' house, I had found something that I wanted to read to him. By now, he was in a complete state of rest and his body was beginning to let go. As he laid there so peacefully, I did all the talking this time. I read him a poem that I had found that week, a poem about dramatically changing someone's life upon meeting them. As I first read it, I thought that he had written it for my grandmother – as he always told the story that she saved his life and that he wouldn't have survived had he not met her. This poem though... I got to the end, and I realized that she had written it for him!! He had saved her life just as much, if not more. He had come along and he had breathed new life into her. They had made the deliberate decision to just laugh and play together every day from that point on. One of my favorite quotes by *n.r. hart* applies so much to their relationship...

"Maybe she needed someone to show her how to live and he needed someone to show him how to love."

That night as I sat at his bedside, I held his hand with my left hand, and I held the poem in my right. As I read to him, tears rolled down the side of his face... and also of mine. When I had finished reading, I played one of his favorite songs and held his hand as we just jammed together one last time. I hugged him tightly and kissed him goodbye, pretty confident that this would be our last encounter with each other.

Permission to Laugh at a Funeral

Pass the Peace Pipe

It was in fact, the last time I ever communicated with my grandfather in any coherent manner. He was kept very comfortable for the next couple of days until he passed early in the morning of March 3rd.

For the past year or so, our girls had handled all of these momentous life events with extreme grace and poise, and we had found a way to soften the blow and break the news gently each time. First their beloved BB had become an angel on Christmas day; then Grandma Ruth had joined the Angel Club just before that next Christmas. Now, their Pappy had also joined the Angel Club, just in time to celebrate Grandma Ruth's birthday with her the following day! We were all pretty exceptional at finding the silver lining in most situations, but the girls really were incredibly mature at dealing with the adversity and accepting what had happened!

We did not have a viewing for my grandfather, rather just a celebration of life where we ate, shared stories and he received full military honors. The entire celebration was heartfelt and beautiful. It was also very real and very honest. We weren't sure how many of his family members to expect, as we didn't know that part of his life very well, and we knew that he wasn't always very close with them. To our surprise, many of his family members attended, immediate and extended family! At one point while everyone was sharing memories and stories, his sons took over the dialogue and had a very open, honest conversation about their experiences with him, good and bad. His celebration of life was powerful; it was real. It was healing... for them and for every one of us who were privileged to be in that room.

My grandparents were really into Native American culture and décor. Most of their home was beautifully decorated as such. One of their most treasured possessions was this long, ornate peace pipe with a tomahawk on the end of it. They proudly displayed it right in their dining room, hanging on the wall. You would never have known, unless you knew, that you could gently take it down from the wall, pack it up, and pass it around, as we did together on so many special occasions.

What better to follow that Celebration of Life than to walk outside together, pack it up, and pass it around. It was the absolute perfect ending to their story and the most appropriate, unifying thing we could think of to do!

Permission to Laugh at a Funeral

Permission to Laugh at a Funeral

Hidden in Plain Sight

During one of those final days of my grandfather's life, I had sent my sister a text message that read:

"I had a little talk with Mom this morning and was reminded that the end to all of this mess is finally here... It's going to be painful, it's going to be messy... But then it's over and I get to start moving on."

Now that it was over, I did get to start moving on. Really, actually moving on and not just continuing to plan for what would happen.

One day as I was cleaning out the endless amount of things that my grandparents had in their house, it occurred to me that there wasn't a single good reason that I shouldn't just take over the lease and continue to rent their place. I wanted to clean and paint, as they were both smokers. Aside from that, I loved the place. I loved the family who owned it. I loved the neighbors. Afterall, I had found it for them originally because of it's amazing, healing ambiance and element of nature all around. I sat there that evening looking around, breathing it in, deciding how it felt. It felt good. It felt right. It felt like it was time. I talked to the owners, and they agreed right away to have me take over the lease!

I had spent so much time looking for a place to rent in that area and then it finally clicked and made the most sense in the world. Often you can't see the obvious thing right in front of you until you're ready to see it, though... and then wham, it just "magically shows up."

I spent March and April of that year preparing my new place and trying to tie up all the loose ends that I had the capacity for at that time. The air was beginning to clear, but it was still pretty heavy. Despite spending some time to myself every night to keep my head straight, I was still surrounded with piles of grief I didn't know what to do with yet. My physical health was terrible, my diet was garbage, I had reoccurring kidney stones, and new to the list were daily full body hives. My body was literally screaming for me to rest, heal, and recover. And yet, I continued to plow ahead, desperate to push through and to be out of the shared house and into a new place of my own where I could really let the healing begin.

One of those loose ends that needed tied up, of course, was telling the girls that their father and I were no longer together. At that point, we had managed to live together for a year and a half, without the girls even being aware that we weren't together. That solidified for me that not much had changed from when we were together for those past few years. We always parented well together and had a pretty evenly shared division of labor. Our struggle was in our ability to connect on the quieter, deeper levels that the girls wouldn't have really witnessed anyway, to be aware of the differences.

Now with a plan in place and a destination set, it was time to tell the girls. My husband was terrified and heartbroken at the thought of those conversations and was more than okay with me talking to them each on my own first, which I had honestly preferred anyway. I wanted that opportunity for a one-on-one deep conversation with each of them, at their respective levels.

I first talked with my stepdaughter. She was about to turn fifteen when I moved out. I remember talking to a friend about how devastated I was at losing her from my daily life. Moment of truth… I never aspired to be a mother, or a wife for that matter. I was never opposed to having kids, but I never felt like I needed to either. And then she came along. I met her just before her fifth birthday and fell completely, madly, head over heels in love with this little girl. She was so smart, and so wise, and so strong. She was funny and silly and capable of anything she put her mind to. All those years later… walking away from her, in any capacity, was breaking my heart. Having an honest, heartfelt conversation with her certainly helped. Questions were asked. Fears were expressed. Difficult topics were talked through. Resolution and reminding that marriages may end, but families do not, was comforting and reassuring for the both of us.

Now it was time to tell our youngest. I told her just before my husband came home from work that next day. After school, she and I were in the backyard painting on some canvas paper. I brought up the concept of what we had already been practicing for months at this point while we were living together. We had "Mommy Nights" and "Daddy Nights" where one of us exclusively handled the evening and bedtime routines, freeing the other up to do whatever they needed / wanted to do. I then told her that Mommy was going to start staying in Grammy and Pappy's old house and that we would start doing Mommy nights there soon.

She took a quiet second and responded with excitement, "So wait... there's two bathrooms there. You mean, we're each gonna have our own bathroom???"

Um... she seemingly could not have been less affected. Her dad walked into the yard a few minutes later, and as she continued to paint, I walked down to meet him privately first, to tell him that I had just told her. She yelled down from the table and interrupted me to say, "Dad... how come you didn't tell me I was gonna have two bedrooms now?!" Bewildered, he responded, "Oh, well... I wanted to keep it a surprise I guess." She continued painting and, in her words, when I asked her if she was okay, responded "I mean, I guess it will be a little sad at first, but it will be okay." And... she was okay. She really did seem to just get it. She knew that we both loved her. She had been slowly integrated into spending individualized quality time with one of us at a time, and she felt secure that her needs would still be met and that her family would still be there for her. The girls were good. We were all good. The pieces were falling into place beautifully, and for the first time in a long time, peace was on the horizon.

Permission to Laugh at a Funeral

Good Friday

With my new place almost ready, and everybody in the know, my moving out was in the near future. One weekend I was caregiving and looking after a friend and massage client while his wife went to visit their daughter. I could write an entire book on that incredibly uplifting and inspiring family, but for today just know that they faced more hardship than most people could even begin to imagine, while remaining upbeat and positive throughout it all. He used to say so many funny things, but my favorite was when he would say "It's not so bad, the short-term memory loss. I get to constantly be excited by good news all over again, and the bad news I forget right away anyway." That's brilliant actually, to just roll with the reality you're in and to find a way to make it work for you. I was always so inspired by that family and my time spent at that house. I did quite a bit of writing years ago when I would stay with him on respite stays - curled up on that chair on their porch in the woods. I loved it there.

On this particular respite stay in April of 2019, I found myself sitting on that chair on their porch, notebook in hand. I knew in that moment that I was ready to release myself from my marriage. I was ready to give myself permission to let go and to embrace whatever would come next.

I began to write; and the magic of it all just sort of overtook me. Before I knew it, I had composed what I called, "An Open Love Letter To My Soon To Be Ex-Husband." At some point, Shawn and I had spoken about my desire to create some kind of public Facebook post when the time was right. We live in a small town, and everyone talks. I wasn't interested in rehashing any of the past year or so, much less my marriage ending, with everyone in town. I could say more, but I say it in the letter, which I'll just let you read for yourself...

An Open Love Letter To My Soon To Be Ex-Husband

Written April 19, 2019

There are a lot of wonderful, amazing things about living in a small town. As the saying goes, a small town is like a big family, and like in a big family, we tend to empathize on a really unique level with one another. We celebrate together, we grieve together, we rejoice together, we protect each other, we worry about each other, we love each other... and we talk about each other. We all do it, for exactly the reasons I just mentioned. We all share stories about each other and add our perspectives to it, trying to relate to it or separate it from our own lives. Having said that, and now that the kids know we are officially separating, I wanted to offer the following as a heartfelt declaration of the love and respect I have for my soon to be ex-

husband. Speaking first to our friends and family... You will never hear me complain of him being a bad husband, he is quite fantastic actually. He is the stain removal and laundry master, the patient bedtime reader, the guy who starts your car in the morning, the guy who will landscape and even get fancy with it sometimes... And you will never hear me doubt his parenting, he has carried the load for both of us this year and simply crushes being a dad! But you will hear me say that I believe that sometimes love changes and our roles in one another's lives change. Sometimes you just can't seem to get on the same page because you're reading from different books... and if I have learned one thing this year, life is Too. Damn. Short. to spend one more minute in a situation you know is wrong for you. And I should add, this is not a decision made out of grief... my mom and I had extensive conversations about this before she passed away. Her heart was broken at first because she loved him so much, but she grew to see the unhappiness we brought each other. She then felt at peace and knew we would be better apart. Shawn was extremely patient and gracious this past year as I grieved and took care of my grandparents, too consumed by life to officially separate. We agreed to live together and share finances and responsibilities for the time being. From this time, grew this amazing, wonderful friendship filled with love and understanding. We know each other's buttons and stop just shy of them and agree to table conversations for another time if needed. It is our hope that our friends and family see that we are comfortable with each other, and as a result they don't feel the need to be uncomfortable with us. We are still great friends. We want you to know that you are all free to still have friendships with us exactly as you always have. When his daughter found out, we cried together, we hugged it out, we had a Q&A and ended up cracking jokes and laughing. She feels love and knows it will be okay. When our youngest found out, she couldn't have been less affected. Kids are wiser than we know, and that little girl has experienced boat loads of love from both of us and has had so much individualized time with each of us that it honestly didn't faze her. In her words, "I mean, I guess it will be a little sad at first, but it will be okay." She fully accepted and embraced the concept, in her words, of "Mommy and Daddy living in two houses and having Mommy Days and Daddy Days... Later when she heard the word divorce, though she got emotional. She associated that word with outward fear... fear that came from the word and not the concept behind it. We held her and reassured her. She felt love from both of us, and she saw how we all still loved and supported each other. She was able to later tell us that it was shocking to hear the word divorce but that she now knew that it just meant the same thing as the idea that she was finding only the good parts in the day before. She has taken the news astoundingly well... and if the one person on the planet that has the right to feel distress about our separation is totally at peace with it, then shouldn't we all be ♡ Oh, and if you want to talk to us about it, it's okay... just be direct, be real, and be supportive. Change is inevitable, but it doesn't have to *be bad. The ending of a marriage, much like a death, or the end of any significant period of time really, is going to be sad in some capacity... but we are choosing not to stay in that place of sadness. We would like to grow & continue improving as we find the joy in each new moment!*

And to Shawn, may you always know your worth and never doubt it. May you find love.... exactly the kind of love your heart desires. May you not spend too much time analyzing the past. There is a lot of living to do right now! May outward influences never cloud the beautiful, trusting, loving, supportive friendship we have developed over time. May we always feel a part of each other's families. May we always maintain the beautiful family that we have created... love changes over time perhaps, but it never faulters, and family is forever. May Stella continue to feel the love of her parents and their mutual presence in her life. May we one day be open and receptive to the members of Stella's family growing as we each find new love. May your daughter see that love can be messy, but that honest communication can make it beautiful. May she also know that I have loved her from that first moment she asked me how I liked her new dress and if I wanted to see her toys. I want her to know that she can trust and confide in me always. I will forever be on her team! May we always be honest and open with each other. May you always know how much I truly love and appreciate you. May you never doubt yourself. You are pretty amazing. May you never stop creating new inventive culinary dishes! May you enjoy every memory you are about to make in that home with the girls. You have worked hard and deserve to enjoy your beautiful life there with them! May you continue to honor my grandfather's landscaping legacy as you dazzle us with your own new additions all the time! Have fun and just get lost in those projects sometimes! May we continue to share in the joys that the girls bring to our lives. May we take time to fully heal, and then take the time to fully develop into our truer selves. May we take the soul searching and lessons learned and find our true loves. May we discover exactly what we want and then wholeheartedly seek it out. And lastly, may we truly know pure happiness every day and may we never forget and always foster the spirit that lives within that beautiful little red haired freckled face bond that we share and how much peace and love she brings to the world ♡

Love,

♡ Tosha

It was Friday of Easter weekend that I sat on that porch and wrote that letter. I wrote it quickly because I had known exactly what I wanted to say. The words had swirled around in my head and in my heart for so long that all that was left to do was to put it in print. And so, I had. I wrote it quickly, read through it once, took a deep breath and posted it for the world to see.

What an immediate and astounding response! It was everything I could have ever hoped for! The number of people who reached out in a loving and supportive manner was overwhelming. Even more though, was the number of people who reached out for advice and encouragement in their own situations, or who said I either gave them perspective about their own relationships or had provided new thoughts on how to approach parenting together after a relationship has ended. Helping establish new norms wasn't necessarily the goal but it has been an amazingly unexpected blessing.

Back home Saturday night from caregiving, it was now the night before Easter. Shawn and I got everything prepared for the next day, and then I retired to the familiar solitude of my own night time porch for a night of quiet reflection before the holiday.

This time I was making peace with moving on. I was wrapping my head around a huge decision that would change everything... everything that hadn't already managed to change that year. It was a necessary change, but it was still a lot to absorb. I was leaving my family. I was leaving my grandmother's house. Tomorrow would be the last big holiday meal I would ever cook in that kitchen. It made me miss her terribly, which then made me miss my mom. At that time, all of my grief was all rolled up into one giant messy ball. Granted, I wasn't moving very far, but also I was moving away from my Dad, at a time when I wanted to be near him most. It was just a lot of change happening at once, and for me, the beginning of a quiet time in which to process all of the life that had recently happened.

I fell asleep that night with a heavy heart and a busy mind. I woke up the next morning and celebrated Easter, admittedly on auto pilot. We did the Easter Bunny egg hunt and basket discovery. I made a light brunch and soon after began to prepare the feast for that day. There were about 15 of us who would be having dinner together that day. What I remember from the early part of that day is Shawn completely occupying Stella and having the most fun day with her playing outside. I was in the kitchen cooking and crying, mostly. Every move I made overwhelmed me with emotion and brought me to tears. I just let it wash over me and surround me, hoping it might bring some comfort.

This wave of grief was too big, though, for that to work. It was too consuming. About a half an hour before everything was ready my sister came in and seemed to have no tolerance for me not being my best self. Don't get me wrong, I love her with my whole heart, but that day in my kitchen, she got under my skin truly in the way that only sisters can to each other. She asked me what was wrong, and I almost collapsed at the question. I said, "Literally what isn't right now? Pick anything. Mom died. Gram died. Marlin died. I'm getting a divorce. I'm leaving this house. This will be my last meal prepared in her kitchen... literally all of the things." She replied back that I wasn't exactly being very hospitable. That was the straw that broke the camel's back, right there. I just said out of desperation, "Why do you do that? Why do you see that I'm on my last string and you just come along and fucking pluck it?" to which she responded by storming out of my kitchen, telling me she was leaving. I'm sure I was unbearable in that moment, too, but very clearly, I was at a breaking point and on the cusp of so much major change.

As she walked out slamming my kitchen door, I knew she wasn't leaving. I knew she would go across the street and sit on my dad's porch until I said it was time to eat. Then it would be like nothing ever happened, which under normal circumstances was how we rolled; and it would have been fine. We've always been a family who felt comfortable and created space to put our emotions on the table without fear or judgment and sort through it together. This day was different though. I felt as if simply breathing was becoming more difficult by the minute. I stood in that kitchen alone – Shawn and the girls upstairs, and a porch full of family across the street, all waiting to eat the dinner I had just prepared. I stood in that kitchen and sobbed hard. I hated that I was in a situation that I so desperately wanted out of yet felt obligated to remain in.

And then it hit me. I am a grown adult who can actually leave if she wants and needs to. It is certainly not the expected social behavioral response, but there was no actual rule or law against it. I found Shawn first and explained to him that I was overwhelmed and feeling exceptionally heavy grief and pain in that moment. He sat with me as we explained to the girls that I felt like I needed to catch my breath and that I wasn't going to be able to do that by staying for dinner. I explained that dinner and the egg hunt would all still happen, I just needed to leave. More than I would have ever expected, they all seemed to just understand.

And just like that, I hugged the girls, walked out the front door, down the steps to my car and as I opened the door, I looked at the porch full of our family and I said, "Dinner is served... and I have to leave." My Dad started to speak and got out, "Oh that's really nice. You can't just..." but I interrupted him as I got in the car and simply said, "I'm sorry, but this is where I'm at right now, and yes I can."

I shut the door and drove away. I felt absolutely certain that I was going to get halfway down the block and feel completely insane. Rather, I got halfway down the block and began to feel the weight of the entire world lift off of me. I had made the decision to end that chapter of my life and to move on to the next. Granted, it happened in a less than ideal, semi-dramatic fashion... but mental breakdowns aren't usually known for their grace or their timing.

I drove around the mountains for hours that day. I stopped at my grandmother's favorite spot, and one that is so dear to everyone in our family. I sat there for a long time that day and made quiet space to sit and grieve her death. I hadn't really done that yet, I suppose. I was holding on to her through her husband in so many ways, and I had been so busy with everything that needed to be done. Now that the major life tasks were over and the dust was settling, I was beginning to really feel the gravity of it all. When I was done on the mountain that day, I drove back to my new home and spent the night there that evening. I called to check in with Shawn and he assured me that everything had been fine and had gone off without a hitch. I could finally rest my head for a little while and trust that the tide was beginning to turn.

That weekend brought with it a Good Friday filled with an incredible amount of public honesty and an admission that this was our new reality. Sunday brought with it a day of reflection, a breaking point, some much anticipated and necessary grief, and the beginning of a genuinely symbolic rebirth.

My only regret that day was not making a plate to take with me before I left.

Permission to Laugh at a Funeral

A New Kind of Normal

When the painting and cleaning were all done, I was ready to start moving Stella and I into our new home. I am a minimalist by nature, but I became even more so during this time. I was grateful to be able to utilize many of the things left behind by my grandparents. I made sure we had the essentials that we use and need daily. The rest... well, the rest didn't make the cut. I was downsizing, simplifying. Only the things that we used and loved most came with us. I cannot tell you how freeing that was! To not only be shedding the heaviness that the last couple of years had brought with it, but to be shedding ourselves of the unnecessary material clutter felt almost just as amazing.

It could be argued that divorce takes almost the same amount of energy to grieve as the death of a loved one. It can tear your whole heart apart. Saying goodbye to the end of a life you worked so hard to create and maintain. Saying goodbye to your partner in the capacity you once knew them. In my case, saying goodbye on some level to a child I had grown so very accustomed to loving every day. But, as disheartening and exhausting as divorce can be... sometimes, it really is the best decision. And like I've said, for us, it was.

We were finding a way to make it work for us so well, though! I have been so inspired and amazed at the number of people who have continued to compliment us, even today, on how nice it is to see the peaceful life we have created and to acknowledge how well we work together.

For example, when it was time to move our stuff in, I didn't have to ask some friends to take time out of their schedules to do it. My ex-husband and beautiful stepdaughter took their evening and helped Stella and I move into our new place. You heard me right... we did it our way. We made the transition to our new life, still as a family unit, just with a different structure now. Those two made several trips back and forth while I unpacked as they dropped things off. After the last trip that night had been made, we ordered pizza and the four of us sat in my new home and shared a meal together. I knew right then that everything was going to be okay. Finding a way to end that chapter of our lives without everyone's world shattering was the most important thing... and it appeared that we had found a way to do that. We had made the very most out of a terrible situation. It turns out, when everyone focuses on happiness and forward progress, it doesn't have to be ugly. It can be supportive, joyful and pretty badass actually! I'll be the first to tell you that I love hanging out with my daughter more than anything in the world... but I LOVE my time to be able to tag out and take a break from parenting! One of us picks up where the other leaves off. She knows constant love and that

her family will always love and support each other.
Again, marriages may end, but families do not. If you
find yourself in a co-parenting situation, try to find
some common ground and help each other get what
you both need from it. It will make you both much
better able to give the child(ren) what they need.

The really good stuff does happen when you're
able to let go of and grieve the relationship that has
ended; to make a conscious decision to start moving
forward; and to build a new friendship and family
dynamic around this little ball of love that you created
together, and both love so much!!

Not long after we separated, I said to Shawn one
afternoon, "Hey, we're both young and newly single.
That means sometimes random things pop up that we
weren't planning on. Can we please just never have to
abide by "your time" or "my time" but rather can we
just communicate about our schedules and hers to
make it make sense in real time?" He looked so
shocked honestly but was happy and agreeable. A few
weeks later he told me that his plans had changed from
Friday to Saturday night and that while he knew I was
going out of town Sunday, he wondered how early I
was leaving. He asked if I could keep our daughter
Saturday night and then he would pick her up early
Sunday morning as long as it didn't interfere with my
plans. I just smiled and told him that I wasn't leaving
until noon on Sunday and that would be no problem at
all. I also thanked him for just being comfortable
enough to communicate honestly with me. I knew in

that moment, it was the beginning of a beautiful friendship; a friendship in which we get to share our love for two amazing little women and to have each other's backs in that adventure.

Permission to Laugh at a Funeral

Permission to Laugh at a Funeral

Deliberate Peace

Everything in our new space felt clean, bright, peaceful, happy. I could breathe in this new space. I could feel that it was an environment, perfect for healing. One Spring afternoon after only living there for a couple of weeks, I was relaxing in this cozy chair in my living room with the screen door open. I laid there so content, snuggled in with a light blanket, gentle breeze coming through the windows, surrounded by complete silence. About that time, one of my new neighbors and dear friends showed up. She came in and was clearly upset. She commented right away on how serene I looked and how chill the vibe was in there. I remember smiling at her and just sort of inviting her gently to match my energy. I told her that she was welcome in my home anytime, but that if she showed up and this is what I was doing, she would have to just meet me there in that moment and unwind for a little while.

That was a powerful moment for me. I was taking control of my own space. I was protecting my peace. I was letting the world know now that step by step, piece by piece… I'll be there when I can, but never again at the cost of my own mental or emotional health. Quite simply, if it doesn't bring me joy or peace, there's not much room in my world for it now.

My neighbor responded beautifully, though. Without a single doubt or reservation, she gently laid down on my couch, faced toward the ceiling, and matched my calm that day in my living room. It was the start of such a deeper, more beautiful level of our friendship!

Weeks later as we were really sharing our stories, she said something to me that honestly just wrapped everything up with a nice little bow for me. As we were getting to know each other, I was telling her what the last couple of years had looked like for me. After I finished telling her everything, she looked at me so compassionately and said, "Damn... you really are going through some shit!"

It was that exact phrase that woke me up and helped me step into my next self. I remember feeling such a sense of peace and freedom at hearing those words out loud. I exhaled and very happily told her that I actually was not, anymore. Without a doubt, I had GONE through a fairly insane amount of life experiences in a short amount of time... but that I WASN'T ANYMORE.

The storm was over. The clouds were lifting. It was time to rest, heal, assess the damage, take inventory, digest what I had learned and figure out who I was going to be on the other side of the last eighteen months! But...more on all of that another day.

Despite a significant amount of loss, my heart and my mind were never more open and ready to process the sadness, ultimately leading to my ability to easily embrace the joy again. Like my Mom woke up and reminded herself every morning, "You have the rest of your life to be miserable, so enjoy today!"

Permission to Laugh at a Funeral

Epilogue

My quick take away from that crazy time in my world is that life is fragile and unpredictable and beautiful. I believe wholeheartedly that we are here to experience it all, to embrace it all. Live life, don't just exist. Connect with each other. Have weird adventures. Make amazing memories.

It is true; I lost many of the main characters in my story, all at once it seemed. But, I am grateful every single day for the perspective that came sometime in the middle of it all, and how well I was able to just be present and soak it all in. That presence is an asset that has carried over with me into my daily life. For example, in general, I am often a few minutes late. It's not intentional. It's not personal. It's just part of my charm, I suppose. But... I can guarantee you that when I arrive, you will have my full attention. Spending time with you will be the thing I am focused on, because the value of such moments is ever present in my mind.

Death sucks. It just does. It is hard to say that ultimate goodbye and to have no real ability to communicate with our loved ones for the entire remainder of our lives. That is a difficult reality to accept, and like I said, it just sucks. It is a reality, however, that we must accept and one that we have no real control over sometimes. Knowing that, let us all take a deep breath and try to move closer toward that acceptance and peace of mind that comes along with the fact that death is inevitable.

Knowing that we must accept the certainty of death, let us also have the courage to control the things that we can while we are alive. Happiness is a mindset and a deliberate choice every day. We have the power to create a life that fulfills us and brings us joy - if only we have the courage to be honest about what we want, to ask for it, and then work hard to obtain it.

As for our relationships with people... we have learned in this lifetime that we can't predict when any of us may suddenly be gone. Say the things. Embrace life. Push fear aside and take a chance. If you fail, but still want it... take another chance. Life isn't supposed to be measured in successes; it should be measured in adventures, in great stories to tell. Some of my favorite stories to tell came from some of the most crazy, heart-wrenching moments in my life!

Leave no stone unturned. Take the time you spend worrying about whether someone will die, and ask yourself what you're anxious about... if there are conversations that need to be had with them, have those conversations. Even if you don't hear what you want to, you will not regret the resolution nearly as much as the eternal curiosity.

Hug your people as if it is the last time you will ever see them. One day, it will be. I can still remember the last big hug my mom gave me. I can still close my eyes some days and feel her arms around me. Hugs are powerful! There is nothing in this world quite like a long hug from someone you're close to.

Embrace life, choose joy, take chances… enjoy the moments when life is really good.

And for the moments when death creeps in to remind you of the fragility of life, remember, friends…

You can do it your way, whatever that means to you.

Give yourself space to breathe. It's important to breathe.

You are not responsible for entertaining anyone during this time.

Give yourself the control to handle things however you see fit.

Ask for help when you need it. There are people standing by waiting for a task.

And most importantly, as with life in general…

Give yourself permission to laugh at the funeral!

Permission to Laugh at a Funeral

Permission to Laugh at My Funeral

~ A eulogy written from the perspective of the person who just died ~

I know this much, if I were here
I'd want one last laugh with you.
So take a breath, speak up and
Share a favorite memory, or two.

All endings are a little sad,
But make time to be sad another day.
Right now all my favorite people are together,
Today we just laugh, reminisce, and play.

I get one last celebration with you all,
A party, just in my honor.
Give yourself permission to laugh today,
And permission to rest your head tomorrow.

Rest your head, and begin to heal,
And when you've caught your breath...
Remember that I am the one, not you,
Who experienced the death.

My story has ended,
Yours, my dear, has not.
Go out and write your next chapter now,
And give it all you've got.

Remember, you're alive
So keep living while you're here.
And remember though I may seem far away,
I'm actually very near.

Life is for the living,
And what a beautiful life it can be.
Give yourself permission to laugh today,
And make one last memory with me.

Permission to Laugh at a Funeral